From Ur to Eternity

1

From Ur to Eternity

From Patriarchs to Spanish Inquisition

1

The Historical Adventures of the Jewish People

Barbara Engel and Diane S. Hochstadt
with Norman J. Fischer Ed.D

KTAV Publishing House
Jersey City, New Jersey

Copyright © 2010 Barbara Engel, Diane S. Hochstadt and Norman J. Fischer

ISBN 978-1-60280-034-2

Published by
KTAV Publishing House, Inc.
930 Newark Avenue
Jersey City, NJ 07306
bernie@ktav.com
www.ktav.com
(201) 963-9524
Fax (201) 963-0102

TABLE OF CONTENTS

SECTION I-BUILDING A HOMELAND

UNIT I – LET'S BEGIN
Chapter 1: Secrets Revealed: Mysteries of the Past — 2
Chapter 2: Time to Date: Clearing Up the Calendar — 5

UNIT II – A DEAL IS MADE
Chapter 3: Who Was First? A Binding Agreement (c. 1900–1700 B.C.E.) — 8
Chapter 4: Spreading the Word: Children Learn from Their Parents (c. 1 900–1600 B.C.E.) — 12
Chapter 5: The Great Escape: Free at Last (c. 1600–1225 B.C.E.) — 16

UNIT III – IN THE PROMISED LAND
Chapter 6: Here Come the Judges: New Leadership (c. 1225–1020 B.C.E.) — 21
Chapter 7: The Kings and Us: The First Jewish Royalty (c. 1020–965 B.C.E.) — 26
Chapter 8: Solomon: A Wise King with a Golden Touch (c. 965–926 B.C.E.) — 30
Chapter 9: Trouble in the Kingdom: The Big Split (c. 926–721 B.C.E.) — 35

UNIT IV – THE CONQUERORS
Chapter 10: The First Conquerors: Babylonia Strikes! (c. 721–586 B.C.E.) — 39
Chapter 11: The Jewish Response to Exile: You Can Take It with You (c. 586–536 B.C.E.) — 43
Chapter 12: The Second Conquerors: The Persian Surprise (c. 538–332 B.C.E.) — 47
Chapter 13: The Third Conquerors: The Mighty Greeks (c. 332–175 B.C.E.) — 51
Chapter 14: Family Feud: The Fighting Hasmoneans (c. 175–63 B.C.E.) — 55
Chapter 15: The Fourth Conquerors: Forever Changed by the Romans (c. 63 B.C.E.–70 C.E.) — 61
Chapter 16: Freedom Flight: The Zealots of Masada (c. 70–73 C.E.) — 67

SECTION II-WITHOUT A HOMELAND

UNIT V – A PEOPLE WITHOUT A COUNTRY
Chapter 17: Skilled Survivors: The Jews Scatter (c. 73–500 C.E.) — 72
Chapter 18: Two New Religions Enter the Scene: Christianity and Islam (c. 1–700 C.E.) — 76
Chapter 19: Different Paths: Ashkenazim and Sephardim — 81

UNIT VI – JEWISH SURVIVAL IN EUROPE
Chapter 20: No Castles for Jews: Daily Life (c. 700–1096 C.E.) — 84
Chapter 21: More Trouble: The Persecutions Continue (c. 1096–1500 C.E.) — 89

UNIT VII – SPAIN AND THE JEWS
Chapter 22: The Golden Age of Spain (c. 700–1200 C.E.) — 94
Chapter 23: The Golden Age Is Over: The Persecutions Begin (c. 1200–1480 C.E.) — 99
Chapter 24: Forced Out of Spain: New Challenges (c. 1480–1550 C.E.) — 104
Chapter 25: Epilogue — 110

DEDICATION

This book is dedicated to
Our dear husbands Stephen and Robert.
For their encouragement and inspiration
And
To our devoted parents
Lois and Bernard, and Evelyn and Richard
For their loving support

Foreword

This is a book with a focus. Its goal is to promote a strong Jewish identity. We believe that Jewish history teaches us who we are. With insight into our rich heritage we hope to inspire the reader to make a proud connection to the Jewish people of the past, present and future.

Jews are often taught "how" to be Jewish but not taught "why" they should be Jewish. Our history tells us "why." It is a story of a tenacious and resilient people who faced much adversity and still maintained their strong Jewish values. These values have set a positive example of ethical behavior for the world. Although small in number, wherever they lived, the Jews had an impact on others.

Two themes are developed in this book. One theme highlights the Covenant made between God and the Jewish people. This Covenant requires many responsibilities and a heightened sense of morality. It is a binding agreement that has sustained the Jews from ancient times. The other theme explores the survival of the Jewish people during their 4,000-year history. Through many hardships, somehow they managed to adjust. By adapting to new situations the Jewish people were able to endure from Ur to the present and hopefully into eternity.

Learning history can be confusing – so many names, places and dates. As teachers of Jewish history we recognize the importance of imparting the larger picture (the forest) without getting lost in detail (the trees). Equally important is a strong organization and an adventure-filled presentation. Using these guidelines we wrote this book to make Jewish history easy to follow and fun.

We are well aware that without knowing the past it is hard to improve the future. We hope that this book will make a special impression on young people as they learn about their Jewish heritage. After all, they are our future.

Surfing the Web

Each lesson ends with a highlighted box entitled Your Jewish World. At the bottom of this box you will find the words **Surfing the Web**. It provides many source materials designed to involve students in historical document analysis.

Such analysis will train students to evaluate ancient and modern political events and movements from a Jewish point of view. Doing this activity can be both fun and informative.

The documents are free and can be obtained by going to **www.ktav.com** and opening the section entitled **Web Resource**. Other Jewish historical websites may also be helpful.

PS. There are numerous Jewish historical web sources which will help you find other documents relating to your field of interest.

SECTION- I
BUILDING A HOMELAND

UNIT I: Let's Begin

Chapter I
Secrets Revealed: Mysteries of the Past

It is always fun to learn more about yourself. Did you know that when you study Jewish history, you are doing just that—learning more about yourself? Actually, you are learning about your Jewish self. You are discovering what your ancestors did and how they lived. You are finding out how Jews behaved in other lands and in other times. If you had been alive in those days, you would have lived very much like the Jews of your studies.

What if you really did live in ancient times? If you were one of the Israelites during the time of the Exodus, you might have seen Moses come down from Mount Sinai carrying the tablets of the Ten Commandments. That must have been a spectacular sight! If you lived during the time of King Solomon, you would have worshiped in a Temple that was decorated with pure gold. Maybe you fought with Judah Maccabee to protect your religious freedom. Perhaps you helped to write the Talmud in a faraway place called Babylonia. If your home was in Spain during the Inquisition, you might have been one of the thousands who avoided torture by escaping to another land. Could you have been one of the Jews who sailed with Christopher Columbus when he discovered America? Imagine how different your life might have been!

Why Care?

Does it make a difference to know what happened such a long time ago? That was in the past after all. Does it really matter? Do you think it's important to know about the lives of your grandparents? Can you learn about yourself by studying about your ancestors? The answer to all these questions is "Yes!" That's why this book explores the Jewish people of the past. They could be your relatives. They could be your great-great-

Many Jews helped Christopher Columbus make his long journey across the Atlantic Ocean to discover America. When he set sail on August 3rd, 1492, he used money and maps provided by Jews. Perhaps many of his crew members were Marranos. Some believe that even Christopher Columbus came from a Jewish family

great-grandparents. Even if they were not directly related to you, their lives have had an influence on your life. Therefore, in one way or another, this book will be about you. Once you discover all the ways Jews have helped to make the world a better place, you will be especially proud of your heritage.

The history of your people is an exciting adventure story. It will take you on a journey to distant places. You will visit Egypt, Babylonia, Persia, Greece, Rome, Spain, Poland, and, of course, the land we call Israel. Along the way you will meet some interesting people. You will meet kings and queens, soldiers and prophets, heroes and villains. You will also meet ordinary people who are just trying to live their lives as Jews.

You will find out that we are a very old people. In fact, Judaism is one of the oldest continuing religions — older even than Islam, Christianity, and Buddhism. It's hard to believe, but today we still speak the same language (Hebrew) and practice many of the same traditions that our ancestors did centuries ago. How could the Jews have lasted for so long? Well, it has not been easy. There have been very powerful enemies who have tried to destroy us. However, we Jews have survived by learning how to adapt, by using our wits, by holding tight to our beliefs, and most important of all, by remembering our unique relationship with God.

How We Know What We Know

You're probably wondering how we know what went on so long ago. It is the job of historians to find out exactly what happened in the past. Historians must gather many facts and then piece them together, somewhat like put-

Solomon Schechter (1847-1915), was a Jewish scholar in Europe and later in the United States. His studies of tattered pages of books taken from a genizah found in Cairo, Egypt, led to an exciting discovery of our Jewish past. He was just like a detective piecing together many clues and facts.

Solomon Schechter examining fragments from the Cairo Genizah at Cambridge University.
Courtesy Jewish Theological Seminary, New York.

ting together a puzzle. They have many ways in which to discover what took place in times gone by. Sometimes, they get information from very old objects called artifacts. Other times, they make use of old writings and records. Historians even learn about the past by examining the food, clothing, and houses of ancient people. Because of all this investigating, you might say that historians are a lot like detectives.

Books give us a good look at Jewish history. Jews have always treasured books, especially ones with God's name in them. When these books become old and tattered, they are buried in a special place called a *genizah*. During times of persecution, Jews would quickly hide their books in the genizah for safekeeping. They also hid official documents, sales records, and other papers. Archaeologists even found shopping lists in a very famous genizah in Cairo, Egypt! Imagine how exciting it would be to find these secret hiding places and to discover books and records that everyone thought were lost forever. Wouldn't it be fun to explore a genizah? Think about all the things you would learn from those old books. You would have to clean off the dust and then fit all the torn pages together. It would be hard work, but well worth the effort.

What if we never found these old, hidden books and records? How could we learn about olden times, where we came from, what we believed, how we lived, and what we valued? As Jewish detectives, where could we look? The Torah! It is the backbone of our religion, culture, and values. However, it's even more than that. It is also a written record of the Jewish people in ancient times. Historians have learned a lot about us from the Torah.

These are just some ways that we discover what happened long before we were alive. It will work the same way many years into the future. What will historians learn when they find our videos, CDs, and computer disks? How will they explain our basketballs, Barbie dolls, and board games? What will they learn from our books? Do you keep a diary? Perhaps 100 years from now it will be found. What clues have you left in it for the historians of the future?

If you live in the United States, your country's history began just over 200 years ago. If you were a knight in shining armor, your history began over 800 years ago. If you were a gladiator in Rome, your history began 2,000 years ago. Now that is a long time! Yet, your Jewish history goes back even farther. Your Jewish history began 4,000 years ago. There is a problem, however. Our everyday calendar goes back just a little more than 2,000 years. Read the next chapter to see how we solve this problem.

YOUR JEWISH WORLD

Summarizing

This book will take you on an exciting adventure to learn about yourself as a Jew. You will discover how your ancestors lived and how they stayed very close to God. Much of what we know comes from facts that historians have pieced together. As you read this book, you, too, will become an historian and a detective. Perhaps you might even solve the great riddle of how the Jewish people have survived for 4,000 years.

Understanding

Did you know that we are not the only people who cherish the Hebrew language? In fact, Dr. Ezra Stiles, president of Yale University in 1781, delivered his entire graduation address to the students in Hebrew.

Thinking

Think about some of the ways the Jewish people have survived throughout the ages. What are some things that you personally can do to ensure that Judaism will continue into the future?

Investigating

Let's investigate your life. Make a large collage that represents your life. Include those things that would tell the world something about you.

Web Resource

Go to www.ktav.com and see the **FROM UR TO ETERNITY** section

Chapter 2: Time to Date: Clearing Up the Calendar

Let's talk about "dating," that is, calendar dating. In the last chapter you learned that Jewish history goes back 4,000 years. However, the calendar we use from day to day covers just a little more than 2,000 years. In order to understand how our everyday calendar came up short, we need to learn how it was created.

A New Way to Count Time

Dionysius Exiguus was the man responsible for developing a new way to keep track of time. How would you like to have a name like that? His method for keeping track of time was invented about 1,500 years ago. And we still use that same method. The biggest problem Dionysius had was when to start counting the years. Because he was making a new calendar, he could start it anywhere he chose. Dionysius came up with an idea. Since he was a very religious Christian, who believed that Jesus was the son of God, he decided to start counting all the years from the year in which he thought Jesus was born. That became year 1.

Dionysius Exiguus made another important decision. He chose to call all the years after Jesus's birth "in the year of our Lord," or "Anno Domini" in the Latin language. "Anno Domini" is usually shortened to the initials "A.D." So the year 5 A.D. is five years after Jesus was born, and the year 500 A.D. is 500 years after his birth. According to this formula, Christopher Columbus discovered America one thousand four hundred and ninety-two years after Jesus. It can get very bothersome to write the letters A.D. after every date. To make it easier, once we get past the first few hundred years, we just leave off those letters. Are you following so far?

Do you see the problem that Jewish people have with this way of counting? Since Jews don't believe in Jesus's centrality to history, using the letters A.D. doesn't work well for them (or for other non-Christians). So, Jewish historians came up with a simple solution. What Christians call "Anno Domini," we call the "Common Era." As they shortened "Anno Domini" to A.D., these historians shortened the "Common Era" to C.E. In other words, 195 A.D. (Anno Domini) is the same as 195 C.E. (Common Era). Do you see why it is more comfortable for non-Christians to use C.E.?

No Minus Here

You're probably still wondering how all the years that came before Jesus are numbered. The answer is really quite simple. Historians could have used "minus" numbers, like "–5" or "–500," for all the years before year 1, but they had another idea. Since the years after Jesus's birth were called "the Year of our Lord" it made sense to call the years before his birth "Before Christ." Just as "Anno Domini" was shortened to A.D., "Before Christ" was shortened to B.C. So, 5 B.C. means five years before Jesus was born, and 500 B.C. means 500 years before his birth. Once again, can you see the problem for Jews? To Christians, the word "Christ" means "savior." Since Jews do not accept Jesus as their savior, B.C. didn't work any better for them than A.D. This, too, was easily solved. Since we use "Common Era" or C.E. for the years after year 1, it made perfect sense to use "Before the Common Era" for all the years before the year 1. So, 86 B.C.E. is the same as 86 B.C.

Here's a tricky question: Which is older, 458 B.C.E. or 316 B.C.E.? Remember, we are counting backwards, before year 1. It is almost like the countdown for launching a space ship. Instead of a blastoff, when we use up all the numbers, we are at the year 1. Here is another tough question: If the first Temple in Jerusalem was built around 1000 B.C.E., how long ago was that? Think about it!

Try more of these fun calendar games:
1. If someone was born in the year 1990 C.E., how old would he be today?
2. If someone was born in the year 5 B.C.E., how old would she be today?
3. Can you write the year of your birth as Jewish historians would write it?

You probably never thought you would be doing math while studying Jewish history! This just goes to show you how many surprises are still to come.

When you study general history, the abbreviations B.C. and A.D. are used. In most Jewish history books, B.C.E. and C.E. are used. This won't be a problem for you because now you understand how this works. You will see another abbreviation in this book. It looks like "c." It stands for the word "circa," which means approximately.

Because our history is so old, we can't always be sure of exact dates. Instead, we know approximately when something happened. That's when you'll see the circa abbreviation "c."

You've probably heard of the Hebrew calendar year that started more than 5700 years ago. What is that all about? Well, Jews begin counting from the time of creation. It is traditionally believed that creation took place over 5,000 years ago. This is figured by calculating the generations revealed to us in the Torah. Using this method Adam and Eve lived 3,760 years before the Common Era. Isn't it interesting that the Jewish calendar counts its years from creation—not from the birth of Muhammad, not from the birth of Jesus, and not even from the birth of the first Jew, Abraham?

You already know that your history goes way back. And that is where we will begin our story. It's time to meet the man who started it all.

A page from a Jewish calendar. Notice the variety of information.

ASTROLOGICAL SYMBOLS FOR THE JEWISH MONTHS

TISHREI — **CHESHVAN** — **KISLEV**

TEVET — **SHEVAT** — **ADAR**

NISAN — **IYAR** — **SIVAN**

TAMMUZ — **AV** — **ELUL**

YOUR JEWISH WORLD

Summarizing

Long ago, a man named Dionysius Exiguus developed an idea for keeping track of time. We still use this method today. Because this method was based on the Christian religion, historians made some changes to make the calendar more comfortable for non-Christians. This book will use the terms C.E. (Common Era) and B.C.E. (Before the Common Era).

Understanding

Did you know that the secular calendar you use in your home is losing time? That's because it is based only on the sun. Your Jewish calendar is based on the sun and the moon.

Thinking

Think about what it would be like to have the day of your birth be the beginning of a new calendar.

Investigating

Let's do something. Watch the moon, as the ancient Hebrews did, to determine the passing of time. When it is the smallest, that's the end of the old month and the beginning of a new one.

Web Resource

Go to www.ktav.com and see the **FROM UR TO ETERNITY** section

UNIT II: A Deal is Made

Chapter 3:
Who Was First? A Binding Agreement (c. 1900–1700 B.C.E.)

We are ready to meet our first Jewish hero. Can you guess who it was? Here are three clues: (1) He lived about 4,000 years ago; (2) he had a wife named Sarah; and (3) he had a son named Isaac. If you said Abraham, you are right! Now, let's test your memory. Do you think Abraham lived during the Common Era or Before the Common Era? If you were paying attention to the last chapter, then you already know that it had to be B.C.E., since Abraham lived almost 4,000 years ago. This is where we begin the history of the Jewish people.

It is time to become acquainted with Abraham, because without him there would have been no Jews. Abraham was the very first Jew. Something surprising and wonderful happened to him, and because of that, we are Jewish today. Soon you will read all about it. Here is his story.

Ur You Listening?

Abraham was born in the city of Ur in a region known as Mesopotamia. Have you heard of the country of Iraq? Well, that is where Abraham came from, although it wasn't called Iraq back then. Ur was located in a fertile area between two rivers, the Tigris and Euphrates. When the rivers flooded, it left mineral deposits in the soil that made it ideal for farming. So, Abraham lived in a land that was rich and plentiful. Not only was Ur near fertile farmland, it was also a bustling city. People came from far and wide to buy and sell merchandise. Life was good for the people living there.

Clay Idols and Many Gods

All of Abraham's closest family and friends worshiped idols. These little clay or stone statues represented gods to the people of Ur. Most everyone at that time believed in idols. It was the accepted thing to do. They believed in many gods, such as the god of the sun, moon, and stars; the god of war; the god of peace; and the god of growing things. You name it, and there was a god for it. Each god supposedly ruled a different part of nature. Every self-respecting citizen

In Abraham's time people built ziggurats (pyramid like structures) as part of their temples. The above ziggurat was part of a structure for the moon god, Nanna. It was built by the king of Ur.

The king of Ur is standing in front of a plant, bringing an offering to an idol.

of Ur owned many little idols, which were put in their homes. Everyday they could see their idols and even talk to them. Keeping these simple clay idols happy was no easy task. If something went wrong, the people believed they had made the gods angry. They thought food offerings would magically fix this problem. Of course, a statue cannot eat, but the people didn't know any other way. This was Abraham's world.

Abraham was unusual because he couldn't believe in these idols. He was sure that the gods made of clay were nothing more than statues. The whole thing didn't make sense to him. He was certain that there could be only one God.

Soon a wonderful and surprising thing happened. Abraham actually spoke with God! This encounter changed Abraham's life—and ours—forever. According to the Torah, God told Abraham to leave the comfort of his home and homeland and travel to an unknown land.

Abraham followed God's instructions. He and his wife Sarah, gathered together their nephew Lot, their entire household and all their cattle. They began a lengthy journey along a crescent of fertile land. Starting from Ur they crossed the Euphrates River, moved on to Haran, and finally stopped in the land of Canaan.

The Torah tells us that God spoke to Abraham again, and gave that land to him. From that time on, Abraham and his people were called "Hebrews," from the word "Ivriyim," which means "those who crossed over [the river]."

A Special Partnership

Another surprising thing happened. God and Abraham made a pact. We call this agreement a Covenant or "Brit" in Hebrew. In order to have a Covenant, each partner had to make a promise to the other. God promised to make Abraham a great nation, to protect his descendants, and to

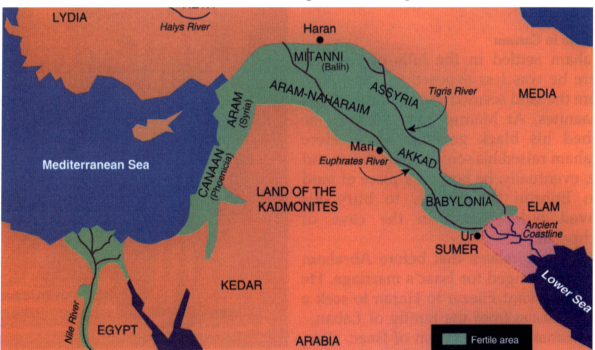

The Near East is the region between the Mediterranean, Caspian, and Red Seas and the Persian Gulf. It is in general a barren, arid area. However, in the midst of this uninviting expanse lies a crescent-shaped region of fertile, watered land called the Fertile Crescent. There the first great civilization appeared and man made the transition from a hunter of food to an organized, systematic food producer. The land of Canaan is part of the Fertile Crescent.

give them the land of Israel. Abraham had to fulfill his part of the bargain by promising to believe in only one God and to obey God's commandments. Now, God and Abraham were truly partners. When this Covenant was made, Abraham became the first Jew.

As a sign of the Covenant, Abraham circumcised himself. In a way, this was like signing a contract with God. Of course, God and Abraham couldn't shake hands, so the circumcision sealed the deal. To this day, when a baby boy is eight days old, Jews celebrate a Brit Milah, a covenant of circumcision. In this way, we are keeping the same Covenant that was made between God and Abraham. Some of you may have been to a Brit Milah. It is a very special and joyous event. Isn't it amazing that Jewish people have been performing this extraordinary ceremony ever since Abraham?

Imagine what an outstanding person Abraham must have been. Put yourself in his shoes. Picture how hard it was for Abraham to be so different from everyone around him. Belief in an invisible God was unheard of in his day. The people worshiped idols they could see and touch. Can you imagine what people must have thought of his new ideas? Abraham even gave up his comfortable way of life and headed to an unknown land because God asked him to do so. What a strong and courageous man!

One Who Cares

Abraham's beliefs went even deeper. He believed that this invisible God cared about people's behavior. What an incredible brand new idea! Idols didn't care whether you were good or bad so long as they were satisfied. Abraham's God did care, and this belief changed everything. For the first time, there was a God who expect-

Abraham by the Jewish Austrian painter Ephraim Moses Lilien (1874-1925). Lithograph, 1908.

ed the people to know right from wrong, who would punish evil deeds, and would reward acts of kindness. This is called "ethical monotheism." The word "ethical" means proper behavior, and the word "monotheism" means the belief in one God.

It was one thing for Abraham to accept one God, but it was another thing for him to convince others to believe as he did. Not everybody would listen to him. Would you have listened? How do you think Abraham won the people over? The next chapter will give you the answer.

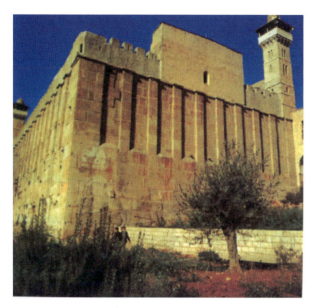

The Cave of Machpelah, where the patriarchs and matriarchs are buried, is behind the ancient walls of Hebron. Abraham was the first patriarch. His wife Sarah was the first matriarch.

YOUR JEWISH WORLD

Summarizing

In the city of Ur, there lived a man named Abraham who dared to be different. He decided it was useless to believe in and make offerings to idols. In his view, there was only one God. This God spoke to him. Abraham understood that this God cared about people's behavior. At God's command Abraham left his homeland and traveled with his wife and nephew to the land of Canaan. There, God and Abraham made an agreement called a Brit. This is when the Jewish religion began.

Understanding

Did you know that the Covenant between God and Abraham was important to the Pilgrims? In fact, they included it in their first major document, the Mayflower Compact.

Thinking

Think about what it would be like to believe in something very different from your friends. How hard would it be for you to change their beliefs? Would you even try?

Investigating

Let's do something. Make a contract with your teacher or parent that outlines what each of you expects from the other. What do you expect of your teacher or parent? What does your teacher or parent expect of you? How binding is this contract?

Web Resource

Go to www.ktav.com and see the FROM UR TO ETERNITY section

Chapter 4: Spreading the Word: Children Learn from Their Parents (c. 1900–1600 B.C.E.)

Abraham had a brilliant idea: there is only one God, a God who cares about human behavior. Many of his countrymen ignored his teachings. They thought he was strange. Yet, Abraham's teachings are still alive today. They live on in the Jewish religion. How did Abraham do it? How did he influence others to accept the Covenant with God?

A Good Wife

One of the best things Abraham did was to marry the right woman. Sarah believed in him, she encouraged him, and she helped him. She was his partner in every way. Together, they fulfilled their responsibility to God by setting an example for others to follow. People noticed that they were generous, hospitable, kind, and fair.

For a long time, Sarah could not become pregnant. Without a child, there would be no one to continue Abraham's ideas. To bring a child into the household, Sarah told Abraham to have a baby with Hagar, her Egyptian servant. In those days, it was perfectly okay for a man to have more than one companion at a time. Today, however, that's against the law and against Judaism. Sarah thought that Hagar would have a child who would be raised by both of them.

As it turned out, Hagar gave birth to a son named Ishmael. He was Abraham's first child. Soon, though, Sarah discovered that not all plans go smoothly. Hagar and Sarah did not get along. Eventually, Hagar and her son Ishmael were sent away from Abraham's household.

A Laugh and a Son

When Sarah was quite old, she finally had a son of her own. Because both Sarah and Abraham laughed when they first found out that she would

The patriarchs and matriarchs of Israel traveled to and around the ancient city of Beersheba,. The Bible mentions a treaty that Abraham made with Abimelech, a Philistine king. The treaty involved, settling a dispute about a well that Abimelech's servants had seized from Abraham. Abraham sealed the treaty by giving the king seven sheep. Some say that Beersheba means "well of the seven," referring to the seven sheep and the well. As a sign of the treaty, Abraham planted a tamarisk tree at the "well of the seven."
Today in Beersheba there is an ancient well near a tamarisk tree, which some say dates from Abraham's time. This photo shows a tamarisk tree with Beersheba in the background.

soon be pregnant, they named their son Isaac, which means "he shall laugh." Isaac followed his father's example, believing in one God. At last, the Covenant of Abraham could be passed on to the next generation through Isaac. Abraham's first son, Ishmael, had many descendants who later became the Arab people. Isaac's descendants became the Jewish people.

It was also important for Isaac to have children to pass on his teachings. He married a woman named Rebecca. She was beautiful, but even more important, she was kind, thoughtful, giving, and smart. When Sarah died, Rebecca skillfully took her place as the female head, or matriarch, of the household.

Isaac and Rebecca had twin sons, Esau and Jacob. These two brothers were as different as day and night. Esau was strong, robust, and wild. He loved the outdoors. Jacob was quiet and studious. He stayed around the tent. It's easy to see why they didn't get along with each other. Their mother, Rebecca, recognized that Jacob would be the better of the two sons to carry on the teachings of their father Isaac and their grandfather Abraham. According to Jewish tradition, Jacob was a willing student. Because Esau was always off hunting, Rebecca didn't think he was the right choice to continue his father's beliefs.

The Next Generation

Even though Esau didn't share Isaac's beliefs, as the eldest son he expected to inherit his father's blessing. Imagine Esau's shock when his brother, Jacob, received the blessing instead. Esau was so furious that he threatened to kill his brother. Jacob then had no choice. He had to run away from his very strong and very angry brother. It didn't turn out so badly for Jacob, however. In his new surroundings, he met and married two wonderful sisters, Leah and Rachel. Remember, in those days it was acceptable for a man to have several wives. In fact, Jacob eventually had four.

It's not surprising that a man with four wives would also have many children. He had 13 children—12 sons and one daughter. They all accepted the belief in one God and the teachings of their father, grandfather, and great grandfather. These are the names of Jacob's children in order of their birth: Reuben, Simeon, Levi, Judah, Dan, Naphtali, Gad, Asher, Issachar, Zebulun, Dinah, Joseph, and Benjamin.

It was a great blessing to have a big family. Unfortunately, in a large family there is often a lot of conflict. One of Jacob's sons, Joseph, was always bragging to his brothers. He would tell them of his dreams of greatness. It didn't help matters that Joseph seemed to be his father's favorite child. Soon his brothers had all they could take. In anger, they

THE WORLD OF THE PATRIARCHS AND MATRIARCHS

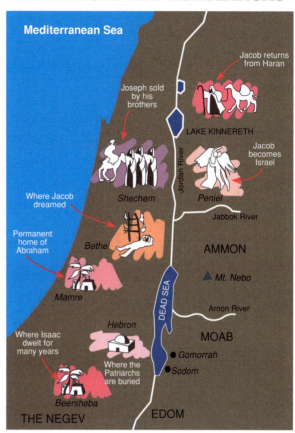

sold Joseph to a caravan headed for Egypt. But what would they tell their father? As children sometimes do in order to get out of trouble, they lied to Jacob. They told him that a wild beast had killed Joseph.

It's a Hard Life

In the meantime, poor Joseph was taken away from his family and the land of Canaan and brought to the neighboring land of Egypt. There, his adventures continued. Even in this new place, Joseph was always noticed. He was smart, hard working, and good looking. In time, he was able to advance from being a slave to being a trusted servant. Yet, his bad fortune was not over. The scheming wife of his master wrongly accused Joseph of a crime. Joseph was thrown into prison!

Even in prison, Joseph stood out from all the others. He had the ability to interpret dreams. It was this special talent that brought him to the attention of Pharaoh, the leader of Egypt. He called on Joseph to explain the meaning of several unusual dreams. Joseph declared that Pharaoh's dreams predicted that Egypt and all the land nearby would have seven good years followed by seven years of famine. Soon people were going to starve due to a lack of food.

From Rags To Riches

Pharaoh was very impressed with Joseph's ability to interpret dreams. He was even more impressed with Joseph's solution to the problem of a food shortage. In order to have enough to feed everyone, Joseph suggested that Pharaoh begin to store food in great warehouses while the farming was good. Then, when the crops began to fail, there would still be plenty to eat.

The next thing Joseph knew, Pharaoh had made him his right-hand man. Joseph was second in command to Pharaoh—quite a promotion for a man just released from prison. He was now in charge of all the food for a whole nation. Because of Joseph, the people of Egypt did not die of starvation.

The Jig Is Up

Egypt became wealthy and powerful due to Joseph's careful planning. People from other lands came there to buy food from him. Jacob, too, sent his sons to Egypt to purchase grain. Of course, the brothers did not recognize Joseph. How could they possibly suspect that the brother they sold into slavery was now such an important man? At first, Joseph didn't tell them who he was. He wasn't sure whether they still hated him. Later, when he revealed his true identity, he and his brothers had a wonderful reunion.

At Joseph's suggestion, the brothers decided to convince their father to move to Egypt. In Egypt, they would no longer have to worry about having enough to eat. In addition, they would be protected and safe because of Joseph's power.

In Egypt

It was approximately 1600 B.C.E. when the family of Jacob, the descendants of Abraham, moved from the land of Canaan to the land of Egypt. At first, 70 members of Jacob's family settled in an area called Goshen. For hundreds of years, they lived peacefully and comfortably. During that time, their numbers grew greatly.

ISRAEL IS BORN

PATRIARCHS	MATRIARCHS	CHILDREN	NATIONS
ABRAHAM	SARAH (Hagar)	ISAAC / ISHMAEL →	ARABS
ISAAC	REBECCA	JACOB / ESAU →	EDOMITES
JACOB / ISRAEL	LEAH, RACHEL (Zilpah) (Bilhah) *Names in brackets are the secondary wives.*	REUBEN, SIMEON, LEVI, JUDAH, DAN, NAPHTALI, GAD, ASHER, ISSACHAR, ZEBULUN, DINAH, JOSEPH, BENJAMIN.	ISRAELITES

They had children, and their children had children, until there were thousands of Jewish people. They were called Israelites, or the Children of Israel. This name came from their male leader, or patriarch, Jacob, whose name had been changed by God to Israel. These Israelites lived in family groups or tribes. Each tribe consisted of the descendants of one of Jacob's 12 sons.

As time passed, new pharaohs ruled the land. The Egyptians forgot about Joseph, who saved them from starvation and made the land wealthy. One pharaoh came to power who was afraid that the Israelites were becoming too numerous and too powerful. Fear can make people do terrible things. This pharaoh and his people were about to do a terrible thing to the Israelites.

YOUR JEWISH WORLD

Summarizing

Abraham was able to strengthen his belief in God with the help of his wife, Sarah. When they had a son, Isaac, they knew that the Covenant would be passed on to their descendants. Isaac and his wife Rebecca continued the teachings of Abraham through their son Jacob. Later, Jacob's name was changed to Israel. Jacob married Leah and Rachel and fathered 12 sons. Abraham, Isaac, and Jacob are the patriarchs of Judaism. Sarah, Rebecca, Leah, and Rachel are the matriarchs. Eventually, Jacob's son Joseph became famous in Egypt. Before long, the entire family of Israelites moved there.

Understanding

Did you know that conservationists warn us that we must conserve what we have, such as food, supplies, and natural resources, before we run out? There were no conservationists in ancient times, which is why there were so many famines. No one saved for a rainy day, except one person. The first conservationist in history was Joseph.

Thinking

Think about our Jewish patriarchs and matriarchs. What qualities did they have that made them special?

Investigating

Let's do something. If you said or did something to someone and you are sorry about it, then apologize. If someone says they are sorry for something they said or did to you, then accept their apology.

Web Resource

Go to www.ktav.com and see the FROM UR TO ETERNITY section

Chapter 5:
The Great Escape: Free at Last (c. 1600–1225 B.C.E.)

In Chapter 4 you learned how the Jewish people, known then as Hebrews, arrived in Egypt. The hard part would be getting out! While the pharaoh who ruled during Joseph's time was friendly, eventually, a new pharaoh came to power. He wasn't so nice. He worried about how numerous the Hebrews had become. To maintain control, he forced them to become slaves.

The slaves worked day and night building great cities for Egypt. The only thanks they got from their Egyptian taskmasters were beatings if they worked too slowly. The Jewish slaves looked back at the time of Joseph when they were a free people, and they longed for someone to rescue them. They also remembered their Covenant with God and believed that they would return to Israel, their homeland.

Rameses II was most probably the Pharaoh who enslaved the Hebrews.

Moses—Our Hero

The Torah tells us that during this time of sorrow, Moses was born. His birth took place just as the Pharaoh issued a decree that all male children born to the Israelites must be killed. In order to save his life, his birth mother, Jocheved, placed Moses into a basket and set him afloat in the Nile river. He was found by an Egyptian princess while she was bathing in the river.
The princess decided to keep the little baby and raise him as her own son. She named him Moses, which means "taken out of the water." Jocheved got a job as his nursemaid and she told him his true identity.

When Moses saw how cruel the Egyptians were to the slaves, he wanted to help them. One day he killed an Egyptian taskmaster who was beating a Hebrew slave. Fearing for his own life, he ran away and became a shepherd in the land of Midian. When God spoke to him from a burning bush, Moses knew he would have to return to Egypt to save his people.

This scene of an overseer beating a slave was found in an Egyptian tomb.

Moses must have felt the weight of the world on his shoulders as he set out for Egypt. He was frightened by this great responsibility, but he didn't let that stop him. He was willing to do something about the suffering of his people, and not just talk about it. He got involved. Moses was a man of action.

But how would Moses convince Pharaoh to let God's people go? Any of the plagues sent by God to the Egyptians should have been quite persuasive, but it took ten of them before Pharaoh would give in. The tenth plague, death to the firstborn Egyptian males, finally did the trick. Pharaoh released the Hebrew slaves, and they prepared to leave. They left so quickly that their bread dough did not have enough time to rise. That is why we eat the flat bread called matzah on Passover, the holiday that celebrates the Exodus from Egypt.

A Parting of the Waves

Now the story gets even more exciting. According to the Bible, about 600,000 Israelite men and their families marched right to the edge of the Sea of Reeds, but could go no farther. As luck would have it, Pharaoh had changed his mind, and his army was coming toward them. What would they do? It would take a miracle! Just then, one occurred! The waters of the sea parted, and the Israelites crossed on dry land. They were safe, but the Egyptian army was not so fortunate. The waters returned just as the army was crossing. The Egyptians were drowned in the sea. This Exodus took place over 3,000 years ago.

If the Hebrews, who were now called Israelites or the Children of Israel, thought that their troubles were over, they were mistaken. Life was hard as they wandered through the desert. It would not be easy getting to the Promised Land. Enemies were everywhere and food was scarce. The people worried that they would starve to death, but God provided manna, a "heavenly"

This picture of Pharaoh Tutankhamen in his chariot was found in his tomb. The chariot reins are tied around the pharaoh's waist, freeing his arms and enabling him to shoot his arrows. The Bible describes the pursuit of the Israelites by the "chariot of the king of Egypt."

food, for them to eat. Still, Moses and God had to keep winning the people's trust, over and over again.

A Sign from Mount Sinai

Finally, after wandering for a few months, the Children of Israel came to Mount Sinai. The Bible tells us that Moses climbed the mountain and returned with the laws of the Torah and the tablets of the Ten Commandments. The people saw Moses holding the tablets over his head amidst thunder and lightning. It must have been an awesome sight!

You have heard of the Ten Commandments, but do you really know why they are so important? For the first time, God gave the Israelites rules of behavior. They now knew that they must be good, just, and merciful. This Covenant, like the one made with Abraham, was passed along to future generations. It was a commitment made to God. Since this was a tall order, the Israelites were given guidance in another way. God helped them choose elders, or wise men. These were leaders who followed the Covenant and set an example for everyone.

Unfortunately, something happened while Moses was on Mount Sinai. He was gone for 40 days and nights receiving the Ten Commandments, and the Israelites became restless. Worried that he was not coming back, the people built a golden calf similar to the idols they remembered from Egypt. They began dancing around it in worship. Moses was so furious when he saw this idol that he broke the tablets. He ground up the idol and made the people eat the gold dust. It is easy to understand why Moses got so angry, especially after everything God had done for the people. Before you judge the Children of Israel too harshly, remember that they had not been monotheists for very long. They would need more time. Old habits are hard to break. It would not be the last time that the people mistrusted God and Moses. They would have to be reassured many more times.

An artist rendition of the Ten Commandments.

1. I am the Lord, your God
2. You shall have no other gods before me.
3. You shall not take the name of God in vain.
4. Remember the Sabbath to keep it holy.
5. Honor your father and your mother.
6. You shall not murder.
7. You shall not be unfaithful to wife or husband.
8. You shall not steal.
9. You shall not bear false witness.
10. You shall not desire what is your neighbor's.

A Second Chance

Understanding human nature, God gave the Israelites another chance. A second set of tablets was inscribed to be stored in a very special Ark made of wood and decorated with gold. This Ark of the Covenant was then placed in a sanctuary called the Mishkan (Tabernacle) where the people could worship. It gave them comfort because it was a place of worship they could actually see and touch. This made God's presence more real for them. The Ark had rings through which long wooden poles were placed so that it could be carried from place to place. This worked well for a nomadic people who were often on the go. The Ark also gave them confidence in battle. Whenever the Children of Israel had to fight their enemies, the Ark would be held up high so everyone could see it. This

Moses bringing down the Ten Commandments. From the Sarajevo Haggadah.

unified the people and gave them courage and strength. It was also a reminder that God was looking out for them.

Homeward Bound

After a few months, it appeared that the Israelites' journey in the Sinai Desert was about to end. They were in the home stretch. Moses decided to send 12 spies into the land of Canaan to check things out. He wanted to know what to expect there. Canaan got mixed reviews from the spies. While all agreed that it was a beautiful land "flowing with milk and honey," ten of the spies reported that the enemy was everywhere and the Israelites were no match for them. Only Joshua and Caleb assured the people that they had nothing to fear.

When God saw the panicked reaction of the people to these reports, He realized that the Israelites still had a slave mentality and they were not ready to battle for a homeland in Canaan. So, God lengthened their journey. Instead of immediately entering the Promised Land, the Israelites would wander in the desert for 40 years. If that seems like an unfair amount of time, think about it from God's point of view. The people were scared; they had doubted God many times in the wilderness. Perhaps it would be better for the old generation of slaves to be replaced by a new generation that would only know freedom. In any case, that was the fate of the Israelites.

The opening words of Psalm 114, which is the Hallel prayer. It begins, "When Israel left Egypt...." This illustrated psalm shows the Children of Israel leaving Egypt. They are led by Moses and are passing through the gate of a medieval town from which the Egyptians are looking down.

19

At last, the time had come for the Children of Israel to enter the Promised Land. Moses died without ever entering the land himself. He was buried somewhere on Mount Nebo. Joshua became the new leader.

The Israelites must have been very excited as they approached the land of their dreams. But trouble awaited them. They were surrounded by other people who did not put up a welcome sign for the newcomers. In fact, the Canaanites were already prepared for battle. While the Israelites were convinced of their Covenant with God and their right to the land, the Canaanites had other plans. Joshua knew that his people would have a fight on their hands.

Up Against a Brick Wall

The Israelites were not skilled warriors. After all, they had been slaves in Egypt for hundreds of years. What did they know about fighting? While the Canaanites had chariots of iron, the Israelites had no fancy weapons. They were forced to become quick learners, and they would have to depend on their intelligence. Under Joshua's leadership, the Children of Israel adopted guerrilla tactics. They would catch their enemy off-guard with surprise attacks.

Jericho was the first city the Israelites attacked. This city was fortified with a surrounding wall. It proved to be a challenge for the newly trained soldiers. They received help from two spies and one citizen of Jericho, a woman named Rahab. With great determination and a lot of shofar blowing, the walls of the city "came tumbling down." This gave the Israelites the confidence they needed. As time went on, they were able to conquer much of the land. Every new victory and their belief in God's support gave them strength and courage. The Israelites finally got what God had promised them—a homeland of their own. Now they would have to learn how to live in this new land.

YOUR JEWISH WORLD

Summarizing

The Hebrews became slaves in the land of Egypt. They built great store cities for Pharaoh while longing for freedom. Moses, a Hebrew who had been raised as an Egyptian prince, became their hero. Having heard the word of God from a burning bush, he knew he had to help free his people. After God sent ten plagues to Egypt, Pharaoh decided to let the Hebrew slaves go. However, as the Israelites were approaching the Sea of Reeds, he changed his mind. The Hebrews crossed over safely as Pharaoh's army was about to attack them. The Egyptians drowned. The Israelites lived for 40 years in the Sinai Desert. In this wilderness, God gave the Torah and the Ten Commandments to the people through Moses. Now they had their laws. At last, they entered the Promised Land. Under the new leadership of Joshua, the Israelites conquered the fortified city of Jericho. The people would now have to adjust to the new land that God had promised them.

Understanding

Did you know that in ancient times no rulers ever provided a regular day of rest for their people? Today you have weekends to relax. It was a small group of people called the Jews who first gave the world this idea of a day of rest. They called it Shabbat.

Thinking

Think about Abraham and Moses. What characteristics did they have in common? How were they different?

Investigating

Let's do something. Pretend you are in a court of law hearing the case against the Israelites who made the golden calf. Take the part of the prosecuting attorney, the defense attorney, or the judge.

Web Resource

Go to www.ktav.com and see the FROM UR TO ETERNITY section

UNIT III: In the Promised Land
Chapter 6: Here Come the Judges: New Leadership (c. 1225–1020 B.C.E.)

What a joyful moment it must have been for the Israelites to arrive at last in the Promised Land. After wandering through the desert for 40 years, they were eager to begin a new life. Unfortunately, the Canaanites did not welcome them with open arms. The Israelites would have to fight for the land that God promised them. The battle of Jericho was a good start, but there would be many more battles before the land was won.

Home Sweet Home?

How did the people adjust to their new surroundings? Remember, the Children of Israel were a nomadic people. They traveled around from place to place tending their flocks. They lived in tribes or family groups which descended from the 12 sons of Jacob. Suddenly, their lives changed completely. Now they could stay in one place. Some chose to become farmers and some chose to live in cities. Although change is always difficult, it was especially hard for the Israelites, who weren't prepared for this new life. In addition, they faced enemies who didn't want them there. These newcomers had much to learn and much to fear. They were pioneers carving out their future.

New Neighbors

You already know that others in the region weren't too thrilled with their new neighbors, the Israelites. While God's Covenant with Abraham promised that the Land of Israel belonged to the Jewish people, the Canaanites and others didn't feel bound by this agreement. They had been living in Canaan for a long time, and they didn't like sharing. But, like it or not, the two sides had to learn to live together.

When they weren't at war, the Israelites

Idol worship was popular among some of the Israelites. The judge and prophet Samuel and his followers traveled throughout the land encouraging the people to hold true to their faith. This impression of a Canaanite seal found at Bethel shows the idol Baal and his wife Ashtoreth. The name Ashtoreth is written in Egyptian characters in the center of the seal. Ashtoreth is mentioned several times in the Bible.

and the Canaanites learned much from one another. The Israelites learned how to fight from people who were experienced warriors. They learned how to make weapons of iron that were very strong. The Canaanites also taught them how to farm. These were valuable lessons for the "new kids" on the block. Unfortunately, the Israelites learned some bad habits as well. Many of them quickly learned how to worship idols, with the Canaanites as master teachers. For example, they were taught how to worship the god Baal to make their crops grow. Sometimes, it just seemed easier to do what the neighbors were doing, to pray to gods that could be seen.

Shifting to Shoftim

As time went on, there was a real danger that the Covenant with God would be forgotten. The Israelites had new lives, new neighbors, and new responsibilities. Would they also start worshiping new gods? How would they survive this challenge to their religion? The answer came with the Shoftim (the Judges).

You could say that the Judges were the right people for the job. Most were men, but, yes, there was a woman Judge. You'll learn about her later. For some 200 years, each tribe was ruled by Judges, who settled arguments and administered laws. They were also military leaders. In addition, they helped the Jewish people maintain their relationship with God. Remember the agreement Abraham made to believe in one God, and Moses's agreement to obey God's commandments? Somebody had to make sure the Israelites kept these promises. The Judges took on that role. They were special people with great leadership ability. In history, timing is everything, and it was the right time for such leaders to make their entrance in our history. In all, the Bible tells us about 14 Judges, but there were probably many more. We will meet four of them. Each one had exciting adventures.

Gideon—The Inventive Leader (c. 1210 B.C.E.)

For seven years, the Israelites had been harassed by the Midianites who lived in the desert. The harvest season was an especially dangerous time, because that was when the Midianites often attacked. They would destroy all the crops and leave the fields barren. For the Israelites, who were new to farming, this was very frustrating.

Fortunately for the people, Gideon came along at just the right time to save the day. He assured the people that they would be successful if they remembered the Covenant. Yet Gideon knew that he would also have to come up with a very clever plan to defeat the Midianites. This plan included some surprising weapons of destruction. Here's what happened.

Gideon gathered together 300 men for a night attack. Each Israelite soldier was given a torch, a jar, and a ram's horn. These would be their weapons. When Gideon signaled, the men entered the enemy's camp while they were sleeping. The torches were hidden in the oil filled jars so it remained dark. Then, at just the right moment, they removed the torches so there was sudden light. They began shouting, breaking the jars, blowing the rams' horns, and making a huge commotion. The Midianites were so startled by the noise and the blinding light and spreading fires that they panicked and ran from their tents. Because they were so confused, the Midianites became easy targets. Eventually, they were driven out of the land. The Israelites learned an important lesson that day. They learned that they could use their intelligence to win battles. It had already worked for them when Joshua fought the battle of Jericho. Surprise attacks would continue to be a very useful technique.

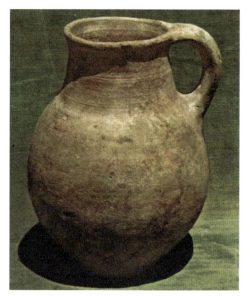

The Israelite commandos threw lighted oil filled clay jars which set fire to the Midianite tents and panicked the enemy soldiers who fled in fright and confusion.
Gideon may have been the inventor of the modern "molotov cocktail". In World War II the Russians used gasoline filled bottles against the Nazi Panzer tanks.

Deborah—The Female General (c.1170 B.C.E.)

Just in case you think that all biblical women were homemakers, it's time to meet Deborah. Deborah was a general of the Israelite army and one of the most famous Judges. She lived about 3,000 years ago.

The Canaanite king, Jabin, had been attacking the Israelites for 20 years. His general, Sisera, had a very strong army equipped with the most modern weapon of that time–the iron chariot, 900 of them! Deborah was the one chosen to rescue her people, but she would need help. Unfortunately, the people were very frightened and she didn't have a lot of volunteers. She did persuade General Barak from another tribe to join her in her fight.

Deborah and Barak made quite a team. Their plan of attack was to climb Mount Tabor and then ambush Sisera's troops, which were waiting below. Sisera probably felt very confident with his powerful weapons, but he was in for a big surprise. As the Israelites rushed down the mountain, there was a huge thunderstorm, and the ground became muddy. Those iron chariots got stuck in the mud and couldn't move. The Israelite warriors were quick to take advantage of the situation. The enemy fled in terror, and Sisera eventually came to a very unpleasant end. He was killed by a brave Kenite woman named Yael.

Samson—The Muscleman (c.1120 B.C.E.)

During those times, it seemed that when one enemy was defeated, another appeared very quickly. Sure enough, when the Canaanites were no longer a threat, along came the Philistines. The Philistines had a reputation for being very treacherous. They lived along the seacoast and they were skilled warriors. It would take an extraordinary person to deal with them.

Mount Tabor, where Deborah and Barak defeated the Canaanite general Sisera.

Samson was such a man. According to the Bible, he was born with special powers of strength. He was so strong, a legend tells us, he once killed 1,000 Philistines with the jawbone of a donkey. For 20 years, Samson was able to keep the peace and carry out the laws. Naturally, the Israelites felt comfortable with such a "superhero" as their Judge.

Unfortunately, Samson learned a hard lesson, and he discovered that physical strength isn't everything. He fell in love with Delilah, a gorgeous Philistine princess. Delilah had a secret plan to find out the source of Samson's strength. Once the secret was uncovered, she intended to pass along this information to her fellow Philistines.

It took Delilah a while to accomplish her goal. She tried many different schemes. She begged and she pleaded, but Samson held on to his secret. Finally, she threatened to stop being his girlfriend. Overcome with love, Samson gave in. He revealed that his strength was in his long hair! If it should be cut, his strength would leave him. You won't be surprised to learn that Delilah became Samson's instant barber. When he was asleep, she cut off his long locks.

Sure enough, Samson suddenly became weak. The Philistines were ready and waiting. They threw him into prison. But the story doesn't

In biblical times lions were found throughout the land of Canaan. The Book of Judges (14:5-6) tells us that Samson killed a lion with his bare hands. This stone engraving excavated from the royal palace at Tel Halaf shows a warrior battling a lion with bare hands.

end there. Weeks later, the Philistines were having a party at their place of worship. For entertainment, they brought Samson along so they could make fun of the former strong man. They chained him between two pillars of the palace where everyone could see him and have a good laugh. He stretched out his arms, and prayed to God for just enough strength to destroy the building. As he pushed against the pillars, they fell and the roof collapsed with a loud crash, kill-

Archaeologists have unearthed the stone relief of the Holy Ark in the ancient synagogue in Capernaum. The original Holy Ark was built by Moses, and was carried from place to place before being permanently enshrined in the First Temple.

ing all inside. It seems that Samson's hair had started growing back and so had his strength. Perhaps, Samson had the last laugh.

Samuel–The Kingmaker (c. 1040 B.C.E.)

Samuel could be considered the last of the Judges, and probably the most important. In addition to being a great leader, he was also a seer, or prophet. In biblical times, prophets were people who delivered God's message. They were

JUDGES

The Twelve Judges of Israel whose histories are told in the Book of Judges:*

OTHNIEL	DEBORAH	JAIR	ELON
EHUD	GIDEON	JEPHTHAH	ABDON
SHAMGAR	TOLA	IBZAN	SAMSON

*The lives of the later Judges, Eli and Samuel, are told in the Book of Samuel, I.

thought to have a special ability to communicate with God. In Samuel's case, he used his gift to influence the people to remain faithful to the Covenant.

Even though Samson had killed thousands of Philistines, they continued to be very powerful foes. During one battle, the Philistines captured the Ark of the Covenant, but it brought them nothing but trouble. Believing that this trouble was a punishment from the God of the Israelites, the Philistines eventually returned the Ark. Even so, the Israelites were constantly living in fear. Samuel knew that somehow the people would have to be united. He did his best to encourage them to follow God's commandments, but the attraction of other gods was becoming very strong.

When the Israelites were feeling despair, the elders came to Samuel and asked him to make them like other nations. They begged him to find one person who could unify all the people. How would he do this? In the next chapter you will find out what Samuel did to meet the people's request.

YOUR JEWISH WORLD

Summarizing

After arriving in the Promised Land, the Israelites had to adjust to their new home. It wasn't easy. The Canaanites and others were continuously threatening them. While the Israelites learned some positive things from their neighbors, they also learned how to return to idol worship. The Judges emerged to help them fight their battles and to remind them of their duty to God. Four important judges to remember are Gideon, Deborah, Samson, and Samuel.

Understanding

Did you know that the president of the United States is much like a biblical Judge? Both serve as commander-in-chief in wartime and chief executive in peacetime. The powers of the President are limited by the Constitution as the Judges were limited by Torah. Yet, both could delegate responsibilities to others; the president to his advisors, and the Judges to the elder wise men of the tribes. Why are they so similar? So many of our founding fathers were brought up with the Bible that they used it as a model for our own government!

Thinking

Think about being one of the Judges during biblical times. Who would you want to be? Why?

Investigating

Let's do something. Create a Web site for your favorite biblical Judge. Include an e-mail address and special sites that would be interesting for the public to visit.

Web Resource

Go to www.ktav.com and see the **FROM UR TO ETERNITY** section

Chapter 7: The Kings and Us: The First Jewish Royalty (c. 1020–965 B.C.E.)

It can be said that the last Judge and the first prophet were the same man, Samuel. He had his work cut out for him when he was asked by the people to find a king for the Israelites. He knew that they were requesting a tremendous change, and he was not sure that the people were prepared for it. At first, he tried to talk them out of having such a ruler. He told them how kings in other lands set heavy taxes, forced men into military service, and took whatever women and wealth they desired. Yet, the Israelites wanted to be like other nations. They wanted a king.

Reluctantly, Samuel gave in. Now, he had the difficult task of choosing a king. He knew that he needed to select a good military leader since enemies surrounded the Israelites. The new king would also have to be popular with the people and committed to God.

The stone remains of Saul's ancient fortress at Gibeah.

King Saul—The Warrior (c. 1020–1004 B.C.E.)

When Samuel met the tall and handsome herdsman Saul, his job search was over. God told him that Saul was the right man to become the first king of Israel. To begin with, Saul came from the small tribe of Benjamin. It was not a powerful tribe; therefore, the other tribes would not be jealous. Also, Saul had already fought heroically to protect his people in other battles against the Philistines. He was simple, modest, and sensitive, and followed God's laws, yet he proved to be a very courageous warrior. It was a good thing he could fight, because the Israelites had many battles ahead of them.

Saul led the new kingdom in war against hostile enemies. Under his leadership, many became brave soldiers. Saul stayed with his men and fought right beside them. He set an example of bravery for them to follow as he led them into battle. They fought against the Moabites, the Edomites, and the Ammonites, as well as their constant foe, the Philistines. During the entire time that Saul was king, the Israelites were at war with one group or another. Yet, Saul brought them both military unity and victory as well as secure borders. He was their hero.

It was not easy for Saul to be the king of a new nation. In his heart he was just a simple farmer. Whenever he could, he went home to his land in the midst of the tribe of Benjamin. He never built a palace, became rich, or had many servants.

Unfortunately, Saul was a better warrior than he was a ruler. He knew how to win battles, but he couldn't build a nation. Perhaps, his biggest mistake was refusing to accept the guidance and wisdom of Samuel. Saul also allowed himself to become jealous and suspicious of other heros. In the end, Saul died in a fierce battle with the Philistines.

A Giant Problem

Saul was most jealous of David, a young shepherd from the tribe of Judah. At first, though, they were great friends. David wrote beautiful poetry, and often sang to Saul, accompanying himself on the harp. Saul liked him so much that he allowed David to marry his daughter, Michal. David even became best friends with Saul's son Jonathan.

Not only was David a talented musician, but he was also a brave warrior. When David was still a boy, he was able to kill a real giant all by himself. The giant's name was Goliath, and he was a powerful Philistine soldier. (Most likely, Goliath was just a very large man, but in those days people thought of him as a giant.)

It must have been a very exciting scene when David came face to face with Goliath. The Israelites and the Philistines watched breathlessly from mountains surrounding the valley where they fought. Each side knew that the winner would take all. Goliath was dressed as a soldier with armor and weapons. David was dressed in the clothes of an ordinary shepherd, holding only a slingshot. Surprisingly, David killed Goliath using his slingshot and a well-aimed stone! David knew that it wasn't strength that counted, but skill and intelligence and having God on his side. He had struck Goliath in a deadly spot. It was a perfect example of the Israelite ability to outwit an enemy. The Philistines were so shaken by the giant's death that they ran away. All the Israelites were thrilled to be rid of Goliath. Needless to say, David was hailed as a great hero, and Saul was green with envy.

A New King

Not only did the people notice David's great bravery, but Saul and Samuel noticed him as well. Saul saw David as a possible rival and wanted to kill him. Samuel, on the other hand, saw David as a popular man of courage who followed God's commandments. Also Samuel knew that God wanted David to become the next king. That's exactly what happened. It was quite a success story. The lowly shepherd boy, David, from the tribe of Judah, became the second King of Israel.

David killed the giant Goliath with a stone from a sling. Soldiers with slings fought side-by-side with the archers. A sling consisted of two leather straps and a stone-holder. The sling was whirled until it hummed like a bee. The stone was then released with nearly the speed of a bullet. It hurtled to its target and could cause death or serious injury. This carving from the time of David and Solomon shows how the sling was used in battle.

Combat and Courage

David had a lot of work to do. His people were still surrounded by enemies who wanted their land. All of King Saul's victories had not gotten rid of them. The Philistines, their old foe, were continually attacking. David needed to put an end to these pests with a powerful defense. He began by uniting all the people. Now, everyone recognized David as the leader, commander, and king. At first he battled the Philistines on his own territory in Judah. This gave him the advantage, because he knew the area quite well. He knew where to fight and where to hide. Under David's leadership, the Philistines were eventually pushed out of the Israelites' land.

With the Philistines no longer a threat, David could concentrate on the other enemies. His armies fought with Moabites in the East, Arameans in the North, and Edomites in the South. Under David's capable command, the Israelites celebrated victory after victory. Because David was an intelligent and able diplomat, sometimes a battle was not even necessary. Negotiations, rather than combat, often settled a dispute with neighbors. David knew how to make friendships and form treaties. At last, the people had the strong king they had hoped for. They were finally building a nation.

The City of David

What began as military actions to defend and protect their land ended with the creation of a large Israelite empire. Jerusalem became the capital. It was the city David selected to be the center of the religion and the government. He moved to Jerusalem and brought with him the Ark of the Covenant. This was a pretty smart plan. Now the people would know that God was with them and would hold them accountable for their actions. David created a major city in Jerusalem, complete with walls and a palace. That's why the city of Jerusalem has a nickname—the City of David.

King David—The Poet
(1004–965 B.C.E.)

David had unified the people, fought off their enemies, established Jerusalem as a capital, and created a centralized government from which to rule. Indeed, he was a great king. To this day, the Jewish people remember him not just for his dynamic leadership, but also for his creative talents. We are told that many of the religious songs and poems in the Book of Psalms were written by David. Since there were no records, tapes, or CDs in David's day, there was no way to record

David playing his harp. Painting is from an Italian prayer book, c. 1450-1470.

The Isareli archaeologist Abraham Biran has excavated the 4000-year-old site of Tel-Dan. He has found a stone inscription which he believes contains the first-ever mention of the royal House of David.

his music. All we have are his poems and psalms of praise to God. We can only imagine how sweet and beautiful his music must have been.

Nobody Is Perfect

As outstanding as David was, he was far from perfect. We all have our flaws, and he certainly had his. For example, he wasn't a great family man. His children from his many wives were always fighting. He made treaties with foreign lands, but he couldn't keep peace at home. In fact, one of his sons, Absalom, plotted to take the kingdom from David even if it meant killing his father. Because of all this friction, he had a difficult time deciding which of his sons should become king after him. Naturally, several of them wanted the position. There was a great deal of arguing, fighting, and scheming among the brothers. When David became old and sick, he finally chose a son to take over as king upon his death. In the next chapter you will find out which of David's sons became the next king of Israel.

The Ark in the Land of the Philistines. Taken from the fresco in the synagogue at Dura-Europos, 3rd century, C.E.

Musical instruments were common in the ancient Near East. This relief from Ashurbanipal's palace shows a quartet of musicians playing a tambourine, cymbals and a harp.

YOUR JEWISH WORLD

Summarizing

The first king of Israel was Saul, a courageous hero from the small tribe of Benjamin. The prophet Samuel appointed him king. Saul was a simple man, but an outstanding warrior. During his reign, there was constant fighting between the Israelites and their invading neighbors. When Saul died, David became the second king. David was a shepherd from the tribe of Judah, who was a talented musician and poet. He was also a great leader and fighter. His armies overpowered their enemies, and the Israelites finally had peace. Under David's rule, the kingdom grew strong and powerful. Jerusalem became its capital.

Understanding

Did you know that the ancient Philistines are responsible for gauze and scallions? That's right! Gauze came from a cotton-like fabric, either made or imported from the Philistine city of Gaza. Scallions are onion-like plants that grew in the Philistine city of Ashkelon.

Thinking

Think about Saul's jealousy of David. Would things have worked out better for Saul if he had controlled his jealous nature? Have you ever been jealous? How did you deal with it?

Investigating

Let's do something. Pretend you were Samuel listening to your friends discuss the idea of a king. What arguments would they make for having a king? Now decide whether or not to have a king.

Web Resource

Go to www.ktav.com and see the FROM UR TO ETERNITY section

Chapter 8: Solomon:
A Wise King with a Golden Touch (c. 965–926 B.C.E.)

Shortly before David died as an old man, he chose his young son Solomon to be the next king of Israel. It must have been quite a sight to see the anointing of a new king. Solomon rode on the back of King David's mule as he was brought down to the Valley of Gihon. There Zadok the High Priest anointed Solomon King of Israel. The prophet Nathan watched from nearby. Can you imagine the excitement as rams' horns (shofarot) were blown and the people shouted "Long live King Solomon!"?

Yet, Solomon did not take over the throne of his father without bloodshed. Many others wanted to have the power that comes with being a king. Solomon was afraid that someone would assassinate him, or start a rebellion. He acted swiftly. His rivals were either sent far away or they were killed. Everyone now knew that Solomon couldn't be pushed around. He gained the respect of the people while eliminating his enemies and staying true to God.

Peace

The rest of Solomon's 40-year reign as King of Israel was surprisingly peaceful. Unlike the two previous kings, he was not a soldier. Yet, he knew what he had to do to appear strong. To show enemies that he could not be defeated if they attacked, Solomon maintained a very large army. He also collected many chariots and horses, which were the tanks of those days. In addition, he fortified his cities with strong walls. The result was that the surrounding enemies kept their distance. Who could blame them? They certainly didn't want to repeat the defeat they received from Saul or David. It was obvious that, if necessary, Solomon's men could fight long and hard.

To promote peace, Solomon had learned something quite important from his father David. Solomon became a good diplomat. He knew that it is much better to make friends than enemies. So, he made friends with other rulers. This allowed him to work together with them to keep peaceful relationships.

Then, Solomon did something even more astounding to develop good will with other nations. There is a legend that he married a thousand wives! Many of them were not Jewish. He did this against the wishes of his advisors. It is obvious that no man needs to have so many marriages. However, these were not love matches; they were political unions. By marrying the daughter of a powerful ruler, Solomon became part of another royal family. You may be surprised to learn that Solomon was even married to the daughter of the Egyptian pharaoh! All his wives and all their connections to other kingdoms made Solomon a very powerful man.

One section of the ruins of King Solomon's stables at Meggido.

A reconstruction of the stables.

Prosperity

Peace was good for business. A friendly alliance with King Hiram of Tyre proved advantageous for Solomon. With Hiram's assistance, Solomon began building a navy for Israel. Soon Israelite traders were voyaging and exchanging their wares for the rich offerings of faraway lands. Israelite sailors told many tales about the riches of Arabia and the beauty of its queen. Even this beautiful Queen of Sheba herself journeyed from her distant kingdom to visit King Solomon's court.

When you look at a map, you can see that Israel is located between the three continents of Europe, Asia, and Africa. Without the planes, trains, and cars we have today, most traders traveled by ship, walked, or rode on camels in caravans with other merchants. In Solomon's time, they were able to go peacefully throughout the region without worrying about war. Riches of all kinds were brought through the Israelite territory and were made available to the people. Traders carried valuable goods, such as spices, ivory, cloth, gems, gold, and even rare animals. Business was booming, and so was trade. Israel was able to acquire metals and precious resources from other lands. Solomon's empire became wealthy.

The entrance to the copper mines at King Solomon's smelter. The Israelites exported copper from the mines of the Negev. The copper was the main source of their wealth.

This potsherd establishes the existence and wealth of Ophir. It reads: "Gold from Ophir for Beth-Horon." The Book of Kings tells us "They came to Ophir and fetched 400 talents of gold and brought it to King Solomon.

Politics

The reign of King Solomon also brought other changes. In addition to the old separation of the land into tribal units, Solomon divided the land into 12 tax districts. These districts were a little different from the old tribal territories. Once a year, for one month, each district had to provide food and security for the king's household. In this way, the king was taken care of for the entire year. Sounds like a pretty good deal for a ruler. It was Solomon's hope that the creation of the districts would also help the people become less attached to their tribes and more loyal to the entire kingdom. He knew that this was the only way to create true unity.

Buildings Bloom in a Building Boom

Now that there was both peace and prosperity, Israel was in a position to improve itself. Many building projects were launched under Solomon's guidance. Whole cities were built to house soldiers, weapons, horses, and chariots.

Large public buildings were erected, as well as new city gates and walls. Water tunnels were constructed to bring the precious liquid into the cities. All this was done using the best technology of the day. There must have been a beehive of activity as the nation was taking on a new look.

It was the construction that took place in the capital city, Jerusalem, that was truly the most dazzling. It took 13 years of constant labor for Solomon to build himself a magnificent palace. No expense was spared. It is very sad that such a beautiful structure was destroyed long ago. Wouldn't you like to be able to take a tour through it today? You would probably stroll through many huge rooms used for entertaining guests, receiving foreign diplomats, or holding important meetings. The walls, floors, and ceilings would be made of only the choicest materials imported from other lands. If you were lucky, you would be able to see the beautiful private quarters of the many queens and the special apartment built for the king. What a thrill it would be to view Solomon's extraordinary throne, made of the finest ivory and gold. It would even be exciting to see Solomon's enormous stables that contained his large collection of fine horses. With all of this, Solomon certainly had one of the most splendid palaces of its day.

A reconstruction of Solomon's Temple.

The Temple

The Temple, Bet HaMikdash, was the most important structure built by Solomon. It housed the Ark of the Covenant, and other ritual objects from the Mishkan, such as the golden menorah. It became the place where Jews gathered to bring sacrifices, and to feel closer to God.

The Torah mandates: *"Three times each year, every male among you must appear before God."* The three times referred to were the holidays of Sukkot, Passover, and Shavuot, known in Hebrew as the *Shalosh Regalim*, or "Three Pilgrimage Festivals."

SHALOSH REGALIM-THREE PILGRIMMAGE FESTIVALS

FESTIVALS	EVENTS	MONTH	SYMBOLS
PASSOVER	EXODUS	15 NISSAN	SEDER-MATZOT
SHAVUOT	10 COMMANDMENTS	6-7 SIVAN	TORAH
SUKKOT	HARVEST	15 TISHREI	SUKKAH LULAV - ETROG

For hundreds of years this Temple was at the center of Jewish life. Even to this day, Jews consider the site where the Temple once stood to be holy. When we pray we face Jerusalem and the long-lost Temple.

Solomon knew how important the Temple would be to the Jewish people. It was his intention to make it a special place for the whole nation. The entire structure was built of only the best materials, and then it was lavishly decorated. Its foundation and walls were made of blocks of stone from a quarry outside of Jerusalem and massive beams of cedar wood were brought in from Lebanon. Beautiful wood paneling lined the inside walls. Woodcarvings, gemstones, and precious metals, such as gold, were used to decorate the rooms. It was truly a masterpiece. People came from all over just to have a chance to see Solomon's marvelous Temple. If you had lived at that time, you would certainly have wanted to visit the Bet HaMikdash.

King Solomon—The Wise

Perhaps you are beginning to realize what a talented leader Solomon must have been. With the help of the two kings before him, he was able to change a simple wandering people into a very strong nation. In fact, Israel became extremely powerful and influential in the ancient world. Solomon was one of its most important kings.

Such success does not come automatically. In this case, it happened because Solomon was very intelligent and wise. To put it simply, he knew how to get the job done.

Solomon was so wise that we still tell stories about him. You may have heard some of them. One of the most famous is about two women claiming to be the mother of the same beautiful baby. They asked King Solomon to decide which one of them was the real mother. After each mother told of her right to the child, King Solomon made a startling decision. He told them the baby would be cut in half so that they could each have an equal part. The first woman was satisfied with this solution. The second woman was upset, knowing that this would kill her child. She immediately asked King Solomon to grant the child to the first woman to save the child's life. "Aha!" said King Solomon. "Then you must be the real mother of this baby. Only the real mother would give up a beloved child to save its life." With that, he gave the baby to the second woman. Can you understand why this was a wise decision?

Yes, King Solomon was very clever! His reputation for great wisdom was known far and wide. His subjects and those from other lands came to him to solve their problems and to receive advice. Today we have some of his writings that prove just how smart he was. He is said to

THE THREE UNITED KINGDOMS

KINGS	RULED	CAPITALS	DURATION
SAUL	1020-1004-B.C.E.	GIBEAH	16 YEARS
DAVID	1004-965-B.C.E.	JERUSALEM	39 YEARS
SOLOMON	965-926-B.C.E.	JERUSALEM	39 YEARS

have authored three books of the *Tanach:* the Song of Songs, the Book of Proverbs, and the Book of Ecclesiastes.

All That Glitters Is Not Gold

As great as Solomon was, he was still human. He may have been a superior king, but like his father David, he also had his faults. Israel grew strong under his rule, but it also grew resentful. His elaborate buildings and construction projects cost a lot of money. It became the people's task to come up with the funds to pay for these projects. If you haven't guessed already, this meant heavy taxes. It also meant that the Israelites were not happy about this burden. They were forced to work a certain amount of time for the king. This type of forced labor is called "corvee" labor. Their discontent was about to change everything.

YOUR JEWISH WORLD

Summarizing

King Solomon was a very wise king who was able to build a strong and powerful empire. During his rule, the Israelites enjoyed the fruits of good political and trade relationships with other nations. They lived in peace with their neighbors, and experienced great prosperity. Many new cities were developed as well as a large and capable military force. Solomon supervised the construction of a magnificent palace. More important, he built an elaborate and beautiful Bet HaMikdash, the Temple, to serve as the center of religious life.

Understanding

Did you know that in ancient times challah was just a small portion of bread dough that God commanded us to give away? Today we call the entire bread challah. So as not to forget the ancient commandment, we still make a special blessing over a small piece of challah dough, and then burn it. We braid challah to recall the 12 specially shaped loaves used in the Temple.

Thinking

Think about the wise people you know. What makes them wise? Is there any difference in being smart and being wise?

Investigating

Let's do something. Invite someone whom you consider very wise to your house for a visit. Ask this person to share his/her experiences with you. Make sure you have good questions to ask.

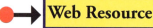
Web Resource

Go to www.ktav.com and see the FROM UR TO ETERNITY section

Chapter 9: Trouble in the Kingdom: The Big Split (c. 926–721 B.C.E.)

There is no doubt about it—Solomon was a great king. He and his father David unified the country, and everyone worked together for the good of the nation. It seemed like the glory would last forever. It didn't. While Solomon had built a vast empire, he was not a perfect king. In order to build the magnificent Temple, he forced people to become construction workers, such as stonecutters and lumberjacks. You learned in the last chapter that Solomon had to tax the people very heavily to pay for these building projects. What's more, the Temple was in Jerusalem, which was a part of the old tribal area of Judah in the south. The citizens north of there were unhappy. They had good reason to be. Solomon was taxing the north more than the south. Samuel had warned the people that kings could do those kinds of things—forced labor, high taxes, and favoritism, so they shouldn't have been surprised.

From Father To Disliked Son

When Solomon died, his son Rehoboam took over the throne. This might have been a great opportunity for the new king to make peace with the northerners. Unfortunately, Rehoboam was not the man his father had been, and he was not a peacemaker. Instead of fixing the situation, he made it worse. When the people came to him with their complaints, he told them that he would be even tougher than his father. He threatened to increase their burden.

This was not a smart approach for a new leader. Rehoboam didn't realize that the people were preparing to rebel against him if their wishes were not granted. He used poor judgment, and he accepted bad advice. Wise elders had warned him not to deal too harshly with his people, but he ignored their words.

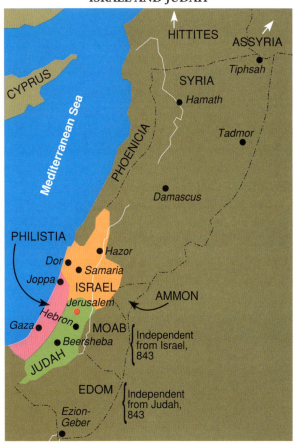

The Kingdom of Judah was also called the Southern Kingdom and its capital was Jerusalem. The Kingdom of Israel was called the Northern Kingdom and its capital was Samaria.

A Royal Split

How would you like to be responsible for the breakup of an entire kingdom? That was Rehoboam's claim to fame. Because of his stubbornness, bad judgment, and harsh rule, the history of Israel took a very bad turn. Instead of continuing to be a unified kingdom, the country would split into two parts. The northern part seceded, or separated, from the south. The result was two independent kingdoms, each with its own king. Now only half the land, the northern part, was called Israel. It was made up of ten of the tribes. The other half, the southern section, was called Judah. It was made up of the two tribes of Judah and Benjamin. Remember that King David and King Solomon belonged to the tribe of Judah. King Saul came from the tribe of Benjamin, which was on the border between the north and south and included the city of Jerusalem. Rehoboam, of course, became king of Judah, where the Temple of his father still remained. Jeroboam became king of Israel in the north. If you think it's hard to keep track of all these kings and tribes, it was probably confusing to the people back then as well.

What a shame that Rehoboam couldn't have been more accommodating. If he had acted wisely, he would have been king over all the land. Now, he was just the ruler of the southern kingdom of Judah. There was no longer a unified country, and he had made enemies with his own people. The situation could not have been worse—or could it?

Secession Did Not Succeed

As soon as the north seceded from the south, problems began. Because there were two separate kingdoms, the good of the whole country was no longer considered. All in all, there would be 19 different kings in the north, and 20 in the south. Both sides were concerned only with their own survival. This was a far cry from the unified empires built by Saul, David, and Solomon. Trouble was sure to follow.

Pharaoh Shishak immortalized his victory over King Rehoboam in a relief on the wall of the great temple in Karnak. In his hands are the ropes that drag the captives from the conquered cities of Judah. Each captive represents a different city.

Each kingdom resented the other, and there were frequent battles between them. Israel, in the north, was certain that it was being treated unfairly. Judah, in the south, never accepted that the northern kingdom had broken away. It felt betrayed. Instead of combining forces, the two kingdoms wasted a lot of energy looking out for their own interests.

THE DIVIDED KINGDOMS 928 B.C.E.

KINGDOMS	FIRST RULER	TRIBES	CAPITALS
JUDAH SOUTHERN	REHOBOAM	JUDAH BENJAMIN	JERUSALEM
ISRAEL NORTHERN	JEREBOAM	TEN TRIBES	SAMARIA

The divided kingdom was also an open invitation for enemy attacks. When other nations saw a country with separate loyalties, they knew they couldn't pass up this great opportunity. It didn't take them long to figure out how weak the once-strong kingdom had become. Have you heard the saying "United we stand, divided we fall"? These words were expressed during the American Revolution, but they fit those biblical times as well. A divided kingdom meant fewer numbers to defend against outside threats. It was predictable that each kingdom would suffer severe losses.

Hysteria up North

The northern kingdom was particularly plagued with problems. The people saw kings come and go, but very few were able to keep the peace. While there were some good kings, most of them were very bad. There were constant attacks by their neighbors. It was a time of confusion. Under these circumstances, it was especially easy for some of the people to be lured away from the worship of God. The worship of Baal and other idols became a frequent practice.

The Bible tells us the unusual story of Ahab, one of the northern kings of Israel. While Ahab did many positive things, it was his wife, Jezebel, who made him memorable. Jezebel was from Phoenicia—the seacoast country north of Israel. She worshiped idols, and she was a real troublemaker. She was also the power behind the throne. Anyone who stood in her way would soon learn to regret it.

An innocent citizen named Naboth became one of her many victims. As the story goes, King Ahab wanted Naboth's vineyard, which was right near the palace. Since the vineyard had been in his family for generations, Naboth refused to sell it. Jezebel, the evil queen, told her husband not to worry, that she would handle everything. She arranged for some people to lie about Naboth, accusing him of being a traitor to

A seal which belonged to an official of King Ahaz, King of Judah. It reads, "Ushana, servant of Ahaz."

The stone tower of Jezebel in Jezreel.

God and the king. He was stoned to death, and the vineyard had a new "royal" owner. Jezebel, in her treachery, had broken five of the Ten Commandments. In the end, however, Jezebel died a terrible death.

Profit from the Prophets

Because of people like the evil Jezebel, it's no surprise that God sent leaders to set an example of goodness. They came along at the right time, just as good leaders such as Abraham, Joseph, Moses, the Judges, and the early kings had in the past. Now, individuals came forward whose only task was to ensure that God's commandments would be obeyed. These special leaders were called prophets. While prophets had been around for a long time, they really made themselves known during the time of the divided kingdom. Prophets were chosen to deliver God's message to the king and to the people. This became their mission.

The prophet Amos begged the people to be righteous and to care for the poor and the weak. He said that God was the God of all humanity, and that rituals alone have no meaning without justice and mercy. Sometimes, prophets delivered their message in an emotional and harsh way. For instance, Elijah believed that the Jewish people would be severely punished if they forgot the Covenant. Other times, prophets such as Isaiah delivered their message in a gentler way. Even though Isaiah predicted the fall of Judah, he also predicted a time when all people would live together in peace. Mostly, the prophets tried to warn those who continued to worship idols that they would be destroyed.

The North's Last Stand

While the northern kingdom of Israel put up a good fight against its enemies, the Assyrians, hostile neighbors from the northeast, were just too strong for them. Israel held out against the Assyrians for ten years, but was finally crushed by the much bigger empire. Actually, the northern kingdom had survived for about 200 years before this final defeat in 721 B.C.E.—not too bad for a tiny kingdom!

You may wonder what became of the ten tribes who were living in the north. So does everyone else. The Assyrians scattered our people to the four corners of the earth. That's why they are called the Ten Lost Tribes of Israel. The only thing we know about them is that they disappeared. Perhaps some escaped to the southern kingdom and became part of Judah. Some ended up in what would become Spain and parts of Europe. Others went to Africa, India, China, and beyond. Surely, many of them died in the war. In any case, the northern kingdom fell, and this chapter in history was closed forever. Although it was looking very bleak for the survival of our people, we still had the kingdom of Judah. What would be its fate?

YOUR JEWISH WORLD

Summarizing

After Solomon died, his son Rehoboam became king. Unable to keep the country together, it split into two kingdoms Israel in the north and Judah in the south. The divided kingdom was very weak. Other nations threatened constantly, and the two kingdoms even fought against each other. It was a time of much unrest. Some of the people turned to idol worship. Prophets arose who warned of the dangers of such behavior. Finally, the Assyrians destroyed the northern kingdom of Israel, and the ten northern tribes were scattered and lost.

Understanding

Did you know that kindness to animals was first practiced by the Jews in ancient times? In those days, it was common for animals to be treated harshly. The Jews did not tolerate cruelty to animals. They set down some rules against their mistreatment. We find these rules in the Torah.

Thinking

Think about how many of the Ten Commandments Jezebel and Ahab broke. Do you think they were equally to blame?

Investigating

Let's do something. Write a letter to Jezebel and Ahab as if you were the prophet Elijah. Tell them how you feel about what they did to Naboth, and how you think God would react to their deeds.

Web Resource

Go to www.ktav.com and see the FROM UR TO ETERNITY section

UNIT IV: The Conquerors

Chapter 10:
The First Conquerors: Babylonia Strikes! (c. 721–586 B.C.E.)

It's a good thing for all of us that the southern kingdom of Judah was not destroyed by the Assyrian rampage. Luckily, Jerusalem and the Temple survived. The people of Judah were very much alive. There was also another group of people who had survived as well. They had special status. These were the Levites.

Way back when the Israelites were wandering in the desert, the Levites were the only ones to reject the golden calf, and God rewarded them with priestly status. They were given the honor of taking care of the Mishkan in the desert. Later on, they cared for the Holy Temple in Jerusalem. A special group of Levites called Kohanim led the worship ceremonies. There was always one Kohen called the Kohen Gadol (chief high priest). He was really in charge. When they got to the Promised Land, the Levites were given their own cities—48 of them—in which to live and serve God. What a deal! After the downfall of the northern kingdom, many of them settled in Jerusalem where Solomon's Temple stood. Now, however, the Temple and the kingdom of Judah were at great risk. After all, the tribes of the north had suffered a great defeat. Would the southern kingdom be next?

The Torah describes the clothing and ornaments worn by the high priest.
The breastplate was inlaid with 12 different stones, one for each of the tribes of Israel.

Holding On

It was up to the southern kingdom of Judah to remain independent. This was a time of constant warfare. There were so many battles and so many deaths. Sometimes it seemed as though the end was near, but then their luck would change and things would improve. Prophets such as Isaiah and Jeremiah continued to warn the unfaithful that they must not abandon God. They predicted that Judah would crumble just like Israel if the people forgot the Covenant. They in-

This miniature from a 14th century French Bible shows the blinded king Zedekiah being led into captivity. Zedekiah's desperate rebellion against Nebuchadnezzar led to the Babylonian invasion of Judah in 587 B.C.E.

sisted that belief alone would not be enough. The Jewish people would also have to behave properly and do good deeds.

You might guess that the prophets weren't always very popular. The people didn't like to be reminded all the time about their responsibilities. Physical survival was hard enough without having to worry about spiritual survival, too. Often, the people were tempted to return to idol worship because it seemed like the easy thing to do—maybe it would make their neighbors less hostile. The non-Jews around them were doing it, so how could it be so wrong? Maybe the Covenant was more trouble than it was worth. These were very difficult times and the stakes were high.

Josiah: Justice in Judah (621 B.C.E.)

Just as the northern kingdom of Israel had good kings and bad kings, so did the southern kingdom of Judah. When a bad king was in power, the kingdom suffered; when a good king ruled, there was prosperity. King Josiah came along at the right time to inspire a new religious spirit in the southern kingdom. He cracked down on idolatry, repaired the Temple, and got the people thinking about their religion again. While he was renovating the Temple, a Torah was found. This was especially exciting because it brought people together from all over the land to see this amazing discovery and to hear it read in public.

For the moment, the people were able to focus on what was positive in their lives. They felt good about themselves. Sometimes it is very difficult for people to change their ways. It is always helpful when the right person comes along with encouragement and direction. Josiah was a leader that the people could respect. The Covenant was renewed. The first Pesach was celebrated since the time of the Judges. Things were looking up, but not for long.

The Babylonian Blast

By now, you are probably getting the idea that danger was always just around the corner. Our people could never be too secure about what tomorrow might bring. Soon, Judah was overpowered by a much stronger empire. That empire was Babylonia. This was the new "tough guy" in the area. Remember Abraham's birthplace—the city of Ur? Ur was located in what became Babylonia. (Don't let this confuse you. In history, names of places change frequently even though the land doesn't move.)

For a long time, the Babylonians had been threatening to conquer the Israelite territory. Finally, along came Nebuchadnezzar, a strong ruler and military commander. Nebuchadnezzar was a man with a long name and a short temper. Even today, Jews remember him because he was the one responsible for destroying our first Temple. It took him 18 months, but eventually, he won the war. In 586 B.C.E., 135 years after the northern kingdom of Israel fell, Judah also came to a bitter end. The day of this tragedy was recorded in history as Tishah B'Av, the ninth day of the Hebrew month of Av. Remember this date

An Assyrian relief showing Jewish prisoners of war playing lyres.

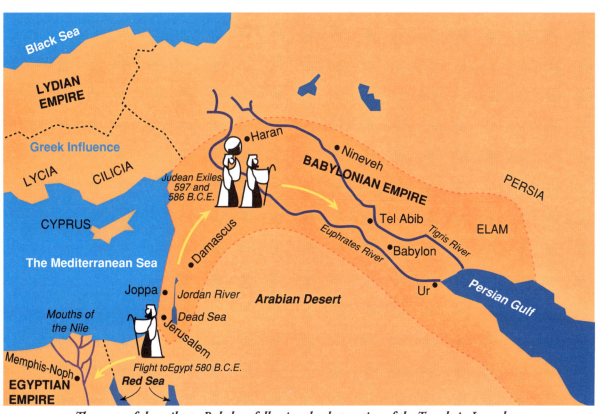

The route of the exiles to Babylon, following the destruction of the Temple in Jerusalem.

because you will hear it again. Isn't it strange that those who caused our people so much trouble came from the very place where Abraham was born? What an odd twist of fate.

A Holy City in Ruins

The city of Jerusalem was completely demolished. The Temple was reduced to a pile of rubble. It is difficult for us to imagine how painful this sight must have been to our people. You remember how beautiful the Temple had been. Solomon spared nothing to make it magnificent—the gold, the silver—all of that was gone forever! The Temple was burned to the ground. But the Temple was much more than just a beautiful building; it was a holy place. The people came from far and wide to worship there. Now where would they go? That was the big question.

THE DIVIDED KINGDOMS 928 B.C.E.

KINGDOM	ENEMIES	RULERS	DESTROYED	DURATION
ISRAEL	ASSYRIA	SARGON	721 B.C.E.	207 YEARS
JUDAH	BABYLONIA	NEBUCHADNEZZAR	586 B.C.E.	342 YEARS

This painting from a German manuscript of 1344 decorated Eycha, the first Hebrew word in the Book of Lamentations. This book was written in response to the destruction of the First Temple. On Tisha B'Av, it is read in the synagogue to a sad chant.

A Homeless People

With the Babylonian conquest, the Israelites lost their land. Nebuchadnezzar, eager to show his Jewish conquests a little "Babylonian hospitality," took thousands of Jews to his country. He settled them in communities along the Euphrates River. At this time some Jews scattered to Egypt, Syria, Morocco, and Ethiopia. They created new Jewish communities. In fact, Jews have remained in these places even into modern times.

Here's the situation: Both the kingdoms of Israel and Judah had been conquered. Our Jewish homeland was destroyed. The Temple was demolished. The Ark of the Covenant had mysteriously vanished. Many of the Jewish people were living on foreign soil. It wasn't the first time our people were forced to scatter, and it wouldn't be the last. Our future looked very bleak, and it seemed likely that the Jewish religion would disappear forever. Could things be any worse? How would Judaism survive this terrible crisis? Let's take a peek at those Jews who went to Babylonia and find out what happened next.

YOUR JEWISH WORLD

Summarizing

While the northern kingdom of Israel was destroyed by the Assyrians, the southern kingdom of Judah remained. Unfortunately, it also faced constant enemy threats. It was hard to withstand all this misfortune. It was extremely difficult to keep remembering the Covenant with God. With warnings and encouragement from the prophets, Judah struggled to survive. Eventually, it was conquered by the Babylonians, and Solomon's Temple was destroyed. Many of the people were taken into exile in Babylonia.

Understanding

Did you know that the Ner Tamid, the eternal light hanging in front of the Ark in your synagogue, is not a modern decoration? It comes from the light of the original menorah that, according to tradition, was made over 3,000 years ago under Moses's direction.

Thinking

Think about traveling to Babylonia after the destruction of the First Temple. What would you expect your life to be like there?

Investigating

Let's do something. Imagine that you are a news reporter covering the big story of the destruction of Solomon's Temple. Interview some people who were there and get an eyewitness account of the events. Perhaps you will want to ask if anyone saw Nebuchadnezzar himself.

Web Resource

Go to www.ktav.com and see the FROM UR TO ETERNITY section

Chapter 11: The Jewish Response to Exile: You Can Take It with You (c. 586–536 B.C.E.)

Our people did not disappear. After all, we are still here! However, the people of Judah who were taken off to Babylonia couldn't look into the future. They couldn't see that the Jewish people would outlast this disaster. You will soon discover how they survived, but first, let's go to Babylonia and glance for a moment at the Jews in their new "home."

Homesick in Babylonia

As you might expect, this was one of the worst times in our history. Our beloved homeland was in ruins, and we were hundreds of miles away in exile. The people were in shock and very worried about their future. What would Babylonia be like? How would they be treated? How would they make a living and take care of their families? Nebuchadnezzar had been a cruel conqueror. Would he also be a cruel master? There was fear and confusion, and many unanswered questions. It was a good thing our people had the comfort and counsel of three prophets, Jeremiah, Ezekiel, and Isaiah.

Although the prophets helped, people react differently to disasters, and this was true for the Jewish captives. Some worried that God had turned away from them and, in their despair, they turned away from God. Others believed that they were being punished for forgetting the Covenant. They felt that concentrating once again on God's message would restore what they had lost. Yet, all had one emotion in common—they were terribly homesick for Jerusalem. They cried by the rivers of Babylon and dreamed of a speedy return.

A Dazzling City

As it turned out, Babylonia was not at all what the exiles expected. The capital of Babylonia, Babylon, was astonishing in its splendor.

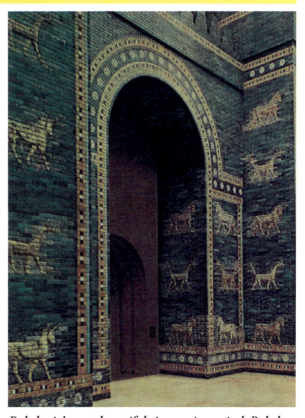

Babylonia's most beautiful city was its capital, Babylon. Babylon was graced with paved streets, gardens, temples, and palaces. Even the city gates were adorned with multicolored, glazed bricks. This is a reconstruction of the Ishtar Gate in Babylon. The designs of lions, bulls, and dragons are made of baked bricks, covered with glazes of blue, gold, and white.

Nebuchadnezzar had robbed and plundered every place that he had conquered, and had taken all the valuables back to Babylon. Who could have guessed that the people of Judah would end up in a city this rich with treasures?

Imagine you were one of those Jewish captives. When you first laid eyes on Babylon, you would be quite overwhelmed. The gates of the city were truly spectacular. They were made of bricks glazed over with magnificent colors. This glaze reflected light from the sun. There were also gorgeous temples, palaces, and hanging gardens. The whole city seemed to sparkle.

Babylon was also a sophisticated city with libraries filled with writings and scholars who could interpret them. Merchants were making business transactions and artisans were selling their wares. Nebuchadnezzar had spared nothing to make his city a show place for the world. Babylon was where it was happening!

Besides being beautiful to look at, Babylon was also a very fertile place, with canals for irrigation. The Jewish people noticed how much richer this soil was than the rocky soil of Judah. They couldn't help but be impressed with such a dazzling city. It was hard not to feel a bit envious of such wealth. After all, Solomon's Temple was beautiful, but it was no contest compared to the temples in Babylon. Babylonia was now the greatest power in the world. Suddenly, our people were exposed to things they had never seen before, and they didn't know what to make of it.

Let's Be Real

Most of the Jewish exiles knew they had to be realistic about their situation. While Babylonia was not exactly their first choice of residence, they decided to make the best of their circumstances and try to start a new life. Besides, they had to admit that if they were forced to live away from home, Babylonia was not such a bad place.

Surprisingly, the Babylonians left the Jews alone and didn't insist on converting them to idol worship. Nebuchadnezzar believed that as soon as the Jews saw his world, he wouldn't need to use force. Sooner or later, they would just become Babylonian citizens by choice. He assumed that within a few generations, the Jewish religion would quietly disappear.

Nebuchadnezzar was right about one of his predictions. The Jewish people did become Babylonian citizens. They became businesspeople, bankers, farmers, and artisans. In fact, they

One of a group of cuneiform texts with lists of the rations for captive kings and their attendants living in the vicinity of Babylon. Among the peoples listed are Philistines, Phoenicians, Judeans, Elamites, Midianites, and Persians. These texts are basic for our knowledge of the treatment of captive foreigners by the Babylonians. This text is dated in the 13th year of Nebuchadnezzar II (592 B.C.E.). Jehoiachin a king of Judah and his sons are mentioned.

became a strong part of the Babylonian economy. But Nebuchadnezzar underestimated the importance of Judaism to its people. The Covenant still lived. The problem was how to be Jewish in a non-Jewish world. This, of course, would be a continuing difficulty for our people even into our own time.

Adapt or Die

At first, the Babylonian Jews stayed in their own little communities. Some historians believe that they celebrated the holidays and continued to study Torah. Soon, though, this wasn't enough to keep them connected to God. Without the Temple, they felt lost. How easy it would have been for them to just give up. The Jewish people knew that they would have to make some big changes in order to survive. But how could they do this and still remain Jewish? Adaptation was the key. They had to change themselves and their behavior so they could live comfortably in the world around them. You may be very surprised to find out how our people handled this situation.

Move It or Lose It

Being Jewish had centered on the Temple from the days of Solomon. This meant that the only place one could worship was in Jerusalem. But that wasn't possible anymore. The Temple was gone and Jerusalem was in ruins. How would the Jewish people continue worshiping when the Temple no longer existed? The situation called for very creative measures. We think that our people devised an ingenious plan. They began gathering in meeting places to worship. Hundreds of years later, such meeting places would be called synagogues. This made it possible for Jews to practice Judaism and come close to God wherever they were. It was in Babylonia that these early "gathering" places were probably first started. If the Jews couldn't go to the Temple, the Temple would come to them in a different way. Now, that's adaptation!

So, they now had the place. But how would they worship? Sacrifice was all they knew. That's what they did at the Temple. That's what their parents, grandparents, and great grandparents had done. What could the Jews of Babylonia possibly do to replace Temple sacrifice, a tried and true practice? We really don't know for sure. One explanation could be that the Jews maintained their identity by developing prayer. Cer-

The writing on a 5th century clay tablet from the city of Nippur. It is a rental agreement from the archives of the Jewish banking and commercial family Murashu. The language is primarily Babylonian with an Aramaic summary.

Eretz Yisrael (the Land of Israel) was the birthplace of the Jewish people. Here their spiritual, religious, and political identity was shaped. Here they first attained statehood, created cultural values of national and universal significance, and gave the world the eternal Book of Books (the Bible).
In every successive generation Jews struggled to reestablish thenselves in their ancient homeland. They made deserts bloom, revived the Hebrew language, built villages and towns, and created a thriving community, controlling its own economy and culture, loving peace but knowing how to defend itself.

tainly, new circumstances called for new action. Perhaps these early "gathering places" and the birth of prayer made it possible for Jews to come close to God anywhere.

Inspiration and Hope

At the same time the Jews were greatly inspired by the prophet Ezekiel. He was born in Israel, but joined the Jews who were exiled

The emblem of the modern State of Israel. The ancient Temple menorah is surrounded by olive branches. Olive branches are symbols of peace.

to Babylonia. In the Book of Ezekiel the Jewish community is described as fitting into Babylonian society while enjoying religious freedom. In fact, some of the Jews did not even consider themselves exiles. The following is an example of Ezekiel's prophesy. It was full of encouragement for his people. He told them that the nation of Israel would be reborn and the states of Israel and Judah would become one nation under one king. That king would be a descendant of David. Ezekiel predicted a future golden age. He said:

My dwelling place will be in their midst,
I will be their Adonai,
And they will be My people.
Then nations will realize that
I, Adonai, have made Israel holy
when My Temple
Is forever in their midst. 37:27-28

The important thing to remember is that our people faced great challenges. Yet, they remained in Babylonia for hundreds of years. Somehow they managed to remain Jews and never lost the dream of returning to the Holy Land to rebuild the Temple. In the next chapter, you will find out if this dream came true.

YOUR JEWISH WORLD

Summarizing

With the destruction of the Temple in Jerusalem, most of the Jewish population was forced to live in Babylonia. This was a time of mourning, but also a time of rebuilding. The Jews began to settle into their new lives and became part of Babylonian society. Impressed by the beauty of Babylon, its capital city, they entered all professions. The problem was learning to be Jewish in a non-Jewish world. They knew that they would have to adapt in order to survive, so they changed the way they practiced their religion. It is believed that they met in designated places, which would later be called synagogues, and offered prayer to keep themselves connected to God.

Understanding

Did you know that parts of the "Amidah," the 18 blessings, may have been compiled over 2,500 years ago. Americans have been saying the Pledge of Allegiance for little more than 100 years!

Thinking

Think about a time in your own life when you have had to adapt to changes. Describe such a time. Was adapting very difficult for you?

Investigating

Let's do something. Make a list of all the positive things about living in Babylonia. Now make a list of all the negative things. See which list is longer. Compare your list to those of your classmates.

Web Resource

Go to www.ktav.com and see the FROM UR TO ETERNITY section

Chapter 12: The Second Conquerors: The Persian Surprise (c. 538–332 B.C.E.)

Have you ever heard the expression "Be careful what you wish for . . . you might get it"? This could have been written about the Jews living in Babylonia. They had mourned and cried and prayed to return to Jerusalem for so long that when their dream finally came true, they weren't really prepared. But we're getting ahead of ourselves.

You already know that the Jews had adapted to their new surroundings. They were becoming part of Babylonian society. They were awed by the beauty of Babylon, and they were even free to practice their religion. All in all, life was sweet. Of course, if you asked them, most would have said that they were just waiting for the day when they could return to their beloved Jerusalem. They were beginning to think, though, that this wasn't going to happen soon. In the meantime, they would go on with their lives.

The armies of Babylon were defeated by the Persians. The Persians were good to the Jews. They allowed Ezra and many Jews to return to Jerusalem. Persian soldiers escorted the Jews. These are Persian soldiers. They are armed with spears and bows.

Nothing Lasts Forever

Babylonia was riding high. It was "king of the hill." Many thought the glory would last forever. It didn't. Imagine the shock, then, when another empire suddenly grew in power. Much to the dismay of the Babylonians, the Persians, who lived just a little to the north and east, began capturing territory. Very quickly they added Babylonia and, of course, its prized city of Babylon, to their growing list of conquests. In the blink of an eye, Babylonian power evaporated.

It had been about 50 years since Babylonia had destroyed Solomon's Temple. Another power had defeated Babylonia. "Now what?" the people wondered. The Jews were especially worried. They didn't know if they would be freed or taken captive. Would they be allowed to worship God and fulfill the Covenant? The new Persian

Inscribed cylinder recording the capture of Babylon by Cyrus.

king, Cyrus II, was now in charge. They were at the mercy of new masters again. They awaited their fate.

A Startling Announcement

The Jewish people needed a lucky break. They got one. As soon as Cyrus II, also known as Cyrus the Great, came to power, he issued the Edict of Return. This proclamation permitted the Jewish people to return to Jerusalem and rebuild their Temple. The people couldn't believe it! At first, they doubted Cyrus's words, but when he even offered to give them money to rebuild the Temple, it was hard to deny their good fortune. The king was actually encouraging their return to the Holy Land. Prophets such as Ezekiel and Isaiah had given the people many pep talks predicting that this day would come. Was it really possible that they were going home?

A Change of Heart

You may be thinking that with this good news, every Jew living in Babylonia instantly prepared to leave for Jerusalem. That was not the case. Actually, most of the Jewish population did not leave. If this surprises you, then try to put yourself into the shoes of the Babylonian Jews who were then quite comfortably settled in a new land. How eager would you be to leave friends and family? How about your work? After so many years, Babylonia—not Judah— was your home. The Temple needed to be rebuilt, but many were asking, "Why me? Let someone else do it!" So, you see, the dream of returning had come true, but there were mixed emotions.

The Jews who stayed in Babylonia continued to live well. Most of them found a way to remain Jewish while living in a foreign land. In fact, at a much later time these Babylonian Jews would become very important. You'll learn more about them in Chapter 17.

A Reality Check

About one-fourth of the Babylonian Jews returned. For those brave Jews who set out for Jerusalem, there was much to fear. The journey would be long and difficult. There were no jumbo jets to transport the weary travelers. Instead, they traveled by donkey, camel, or on foot. The trip would take several months through many miles of desert and rugged terrain.

When they arrived, it must have been very disturbing to see their precious Jerusalem in

The tomb of Cyrus, who allowed the Jews to return to Jerusalem.

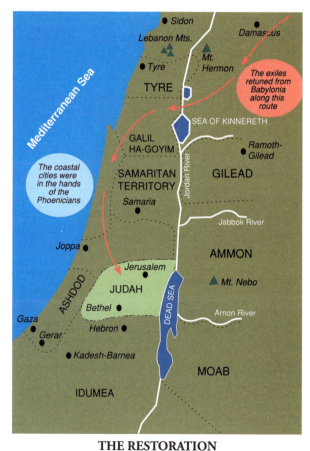

THE RESTORATION
Cyrus was a liberal ruler and allowed the worship of the God of Israel in Jerusalem.

ruins. Where would they live? How would they feed their families? They knew that their work was cut out for them. It was one thing to dream about rebuilding the Temple; it was another to actually do it. To add to their troubles, there was still plenty of fighting going on with neighboring people, such as the Samaritans. Though it would be difficult, the new Temple building project would soon begin.

A New Beginning

The tedious task of rebuilding began. Finally, in the year 515 B.C.E., more than 20 years after returning to Jerusalem the second Temple was completed. Because of limited funds and a small workforce, the Second Temple could not compare in beauty to Solomon's Temple. Yet, this labor of love was completed. The people had come together to rebuild their Temple and their lives. There was much rejoicing, but most knew that more work was still ahead.

Spiritually, the Jews had lost much. Sadly, there were few who could remember the Torah—the laws of God. Another problem was more practical, and had to do with self-defense. Jerusalem was a very easy target for warring nations because the city had no fortifications.

Meanwhile, in Babylonia, two very important heroes were about to make the long journey back to Jerusalem. These were not ordinary men. They were pioneers who knew that the time for action had come. They had heard reports that their people were struggling, and they prepared to come to the rescue. Both would make a big difference in the survival of our people. Let's meet them.

Ezra and Nehemiah: A Time for Rebuilding

Ezra was a great religious leader who was living in Babylonia. When he discovered that the

Hebrew coin dating back to the 4th century B.C.E. the period of Ezra the Scribe. The coin is inscribe YHD (in ancient Hebrew script), which stands for Yehud, the Persian name of Judea.

Jewish community in Jerusalem was in need of a spiritual boost, he knew he could help. He decided to leave his comfortable home and make the pilgrimage to the Holy Land. He brought with him another 1,500 Jews who were also eager to return.

Soon after Ezra arrived, it became clear to him that the people needed to refresh their ties to the Torah. He had to find some way to reconnect them to God's laws and make the Torah part of everyday life. A decision was made to have public readings of the Torah on Mondays, and Thursdays. These readings were in addition to the Torah readings on Saturday mornings. This turned out to be a great idea. The Jews began studying together on a regular basis.

Now that the Jews in Jerusalem had a spiritual leader, they would need someone to manage their daily affairs. Nehemiah became the new governor. His first order of business was to rebuild the walls around the city so that Jerusalem wouldn't be defenseless against its enemies. Just as important, Nehemiah made some changes in the way people treated others. He established laws protecting basic human rights. These laws, of course, were all based on the teachings of Torah. Both Ezra and Nehemiah encouraged strict observance of the Sabbath and discouraged marriages with foreigners. They were hoping that this would ensure the continuance of the Jewish people.

Soon, there was a new feeling of rebirth. The next 200 years brought peace. The people were again connecting with God. In Babylon, the Jews had discovered how to remain Jewish. They learned a lot about adaptation and survival. They had survived the Babylonians and the Persians. Who would be next? You are probably seeing a pattern develop, so you won't be too surprised to learn that new conquerors would eventually be on their way to end this peaceful time. These new conquerors would present a challenge to our people that had not been encountered before.

YOUR JEWISH WORLD

Summarizing

The Jews living in Babylonia had adapted well to their new home. While they still longed to return to Jerusalem, they had settled into a comfortable life. When the Babylonian empire was conquered by the Persian king, Cyrus the Great, the Jews were allowed to return and rebuild their Temple. Only about one-fourth returned. When they arrived, they saw a city in ruins. They began the tedious job of rebuilding. Some years later, two men helped revive Jerusalem. They were Ezra and Nehemiah. Through their efforts the people soon began to connect again with God.

Understanding

Did you know that you can thank Ezra that you are offered a public education? Well, actually, he was the first one to gather all the people together to learn Torah, the laws, and the history of the Jewish people. Before him, only a special few were educated.

Thinking

Think about the Jews who returned to Jerusalem from Babylonia to rebuild the Temple. Would you have stayed in Babylonia, or would you have returned? Why?

Investigating

Let's do something. Survey your friends and family. Ask them if they would have returned to Jerusalem, or stayed in Babylonia. Make sure to give them all the facts. Evaluate the results of their answers.

Web Resource

Go to www.ktav.com and see the
FROM UR TO ETERNITY section

Chapter 13: The Third Conquerors: The Mighty Greeks (c. 332–175 B.C.E.)

The year was 332 B.C.E. A new leader with tremendous might defeated the weakening Persian Empire, including Jerusalem. Here we go again! The Jews had another new ruler. He was a brilliant general from Macedonia, in northern Greece. His troops marched through the territories we now call Turkey, Syria, Israel, Egypt, Iraq, Iran, Afghanistan, and Pakistan. This was a huge area, and he conquered it all. Who was this bold man who led such a powerful force? His name was Alexander the Great.

In less than ten years after establishing this large empire, Alexander the Great became ill and died. He was only 33 years old. Isn't it amazing what he was able to accomplish in such a short lifetime? Even more amazing, the Jewish people were not at all unhappy under his rule. You see, he allowed them to continue their way of life. He didn't interfere with their religious practices. In fact, he admired and respected Jews and Judaism. Many Jews even named their children after him.

Doing the Splits

In a way, Alexander the Great left behind a kingdom without a king. Think of the confusion this must have caused. His military generals immediately recognized their chance to gain their own power. For several years, they fought against one another. The result was the eventual splitting of the Greek empire into three areas. One general controlled the homeland of Greece. Another, Seleucus, took over Babylonia, Persia, and Syria. The third general, Ptolemy, became the ruler of Egypt and Judea. Judea is the name the Greeks gave to Judah, the land occupied by the Israelites. By the way the word Jew comes from the name of Jacob's fourth son, Judah.

A mosaic showing a likeness of Alexander the Great.

Despite all the power struggles and the eventual rule of Ptolemy, life continued much the same for the Jewish people. They still didn't have an independent nation and still had to pay taxes to a foreign government. This was nothing new; they were used to that. However, their situation wasn't all bad. They were allowed to keep their own language, practice their own religion, and live under the direct control of their own leaders. Do you remember learning about the Kohen Gadol? He was the chief religious leader, the head of all the Levites. The Greeks appointed him to be the head of the local government. In turn, he reported to the Greek authorities. The Jewish citizens selected his assistants. Doesn't this seem much like our own democracy in which we choose our own representatives?

Alexander the Great being greeted by the High Priest Jaddua. From a 14th century French picture.

Killing Us with Kindness

The Jews were accustomed to being controlled by other nations, but none were quite like the Greeks. Life was almost too good. What was going on? The answer is that the Greeks were clever. Rather than force changes upon the conquered people, they slowly introduced the Greek way of life into their land. It all started with Alexander the Great. As soon as he conquered the land, he began populating it with his own people. He actually ordered his soldiers to choose wives from the local residents. In this way, the Greeks quickly became a part of the general population. They mixed right in. It was an absolutely brilliant way to spread Greek influence and culture.

In addition to this, Jews were welcomed into other areas of the Greek Empire. They began to settle in many different places. A thriving Jewish community developed in Alexandria, a city in Egypt. Can you guess why it was named Alexandria? Here Jews lived happily and comfortably. They easily blended into the rest of society. At the same time, they were gradually becoming more and more like the Greeks. We call this assimilation.

Can You Say "Septuagint"?

The Greeks were fascinated with Judaism. It is said that even Alexander the Great visited the Temple to learn more about the Jewish religion. The Greek people had never come across another nation quite like Judea. Certainly, they never met a people so devoted to just one God. Their natural curiosity about Jewish thought and practices led them to the Torah. They wanted to learn about its teachings in order to discover why it was so important to the Jews. There was just one problem. The Greeks could not read Hebrew, the language of the Torah.

In 265 B.C.E., Ptolemy II, the Greek ruler living in Alexandria, decided to have the Torah translated from Hebrew to Greek. Legend has it that he asked each of the 12 tribes of Israel to send six of their best Jewish scholars to Alexandria. When they arrived, he gave each of them a separate room and asked them to translate the Torah into Greek. Amazingly, each translation was exactly like the next, even though the scholars were not allowed to work together. This translation of the Torah is known as the Septuagint, which means "seventy." The name refers to the 72 translators. This was the first time the books of the Torah were written in a language other than Hebrew.

It's All Greek to Me

The Jews were fascinated with the Greeks, just as the Greeks were fascinated with the Jews. The Greeks had a very rich culture. They were highly intellectual, deep thinkers—just like the Jews. They valued learning and developed academies of higher education. They debated ideas and created new scientific theories. The famous philosophers Socrates, Plato, and Aristotle were all Greek. The Greeks also mastered the arts. They were accomplished writers, poets, actors, sculptors, and architects. How awesome!

If that wasn't enough, the Greeks also loved sports. Athletic competition became a very important part of the Greek way of life. Young boys would train to become outstanding discus throwers, wrestlers, or runners. You probably know that the first Olympic games were held in Greece. These games were just another way to show how the human body could become really perfect with practice. If there had been exercise clubs back then, the Greeks would have been the first to join. Perhaps it is the lasting Greek influence that causes Americans to pay so much attention to the Super Bowl, the World Series, and the Stanley Cup. What do you think?

The Jewish people had never been exposed to such an advanced culture. It was exciting and stimulating to them. You can almost predict what happened. Before long, Jews began to copy the Greek ways. Their children were given Greek names. They even began to look like the Greeks. They dressed in Greek clothing and wore Greek hairstyles. In order to study Greek books, they learned the Greek language. They studied Greek philosophy, science, and literature. Slowly, many Jews and Greeks began to look and act the same.

Hello Hellenism

The admiration and imitation of the Greek ways was called "Hellenism." This name comes from the word "Hellenes," the name the Greeks called themselves. There was nothing wrong with the Jews learning from the Greeks, but some took it too far. They adopted the entire Greek way of life—both the good and the bad. These Jews were called "Hellenists." They slowly became more Greek than Jewish.

Although the Greeks had a lot of good ideas, some of their beliefs were not acceptable to Judaism. For example, the Greeks worshiped many gods. They loved telling tall tales about them. One story you may have heard concerns the muscular god Atlas who holds the entire

A page from the Septuagint, Exodus 19.

world on his shoulders.

You already know that the Greeks admired strength and loved sports. Jews also appreciated strong bodies, but were more concerned with strong character. Whereas Hellenism put value on the beauty of the body, Judaism put value on the beauty of the soul. It's a big difference! Besides, ancient Greeks owned slaves as property, treated others cruelly, and thought only of their own well being. Many of them pampered themselves by eating big meals, getting drunk, and having wild parties. Their own personal pleasures were more important then anything else. Are you beginning to see the conflict between the Greeks and the Jews?

In time, there developed a deep division among the Jewish people. The clash was between those who held fast to Judaism, and those who became Hellenists. As you probably know, it is quite tough to resist doing the popular thing even when you know that it is wrong. Devoted Jews were being put to the test. For the most part, Jews maintained their belief in God and kept the laws of the Torah. Fortunately, the Jewish people did not disappear into Greek society. Instead, they learned how to live surrounded by other ideas and influences while keeping their own beliefs. This would very quickly become an important skill. It would not be long before the Greeks would test the Jewish way of life in yet another manner.

A Greek relief of naked wrestlers at a gymnasium. The gymnasium was a sport stadium where games and concerts were held. Before an exhibition there was a special opening ceremony in which the athletes paraded naked and then offered sacrifices to the pagan gods. To the Greeks, it was a way of life. To the Jews, it was a road to idol worship and assimilation.

YOUR JEWISH WORLD

Summarizing

The Greeks were the third powerful nation to conquer Judah. A capable general named Alexander the Great was their leader. Upon his death, Judah came under the authority of the Greek ruler of Egypt. The Jewish people were allowed to maintain their way of life and keep their religious practices. They were even encouraged to settle in other Greek cities, such as Alexandria, Egypt. There was a great deal of admiration between the Greeks and Jews. Both nations appreciated scholarship and intellect, but their values and religious beliefs were very different. The Greeks particularly admired the Jewish devotion to the Torah. To learn what it said, the Torah was translated from Hebrew to Greek. This translation is called the Septuagint. Gradually, more and more Jews began to live and act like the Greeks. These Jews were called Hellenists. The new threat to Judaism was assimilation. Yet, most Jews maintained their strong religious beliefs.

Understanding

Did you know that recycling is not new to the Jews? The Talmud talks about Bal Tashchit, which means "do not destroy." This is a Jewish value. It focuses on not wasting things that can help others. Many today are concerned about protecting our world. Jews have had this concern for thousands of years.

Thinking

Think about ways your Jewish beliefs have been tested, challenged, and influenced by the non-Jews you know. Do you think the Jews living in the ancient Greek Empire had similar experiences?

Investigating

Let's do something. Draw a cartoon showing Alexander the Great entering Jerusalem.

Web Resource

Go to www.ktav.com and see the FROM UR TO ETERNITY section

Chapter 14: Family Feud: The Fighting Hasmoneans (c. 175–63 B.C.E.)

A hundred years went by before Judea experienced another change of ruling families. This time there was a power struggle between two Greek rulers. If you remember, three kingdoms were created when the Greeks divided the land which Alexander the Great had conquered. Judea was caught between the Ptolemaic rule in Egypt to the south and the Seleucid rule in Syria to the north. Both kingdoms were very jealous of the territory of the other. Eventually, the Seleucid king successfully grabbed control of Judea.

The Jewish people now had a different king ruling over them. At first, there was very little difference between the rule of the Ptolemaic and Seleucid kings. Their new king was eager for the Jews to be content with his authority. The Jews were allowed to keep their religious practices just as before. In fact, the Jews were given a guarantee that they could continue to have religious freedom. To make them even happier, their taxes were reduced. As long as there was a kind and generous Seleucid king in power, the people of Judea had no problems. However, a change was on the way.

New Power Brings New Problems

In a few years, another king took over the throne. His name was Antiochus IV Epiphanes. The Judeans liked to call him Antiochus Epimanes—meaning "Antiochus the mad man." During his harsh rule, the stage was set for the events that led up to the holiday of Chanukah.

Antiochus had dreams of glory. Such dreams cost money, so he doubled the taxes. To get even more funds, the rich treasures of the Temple were taken by the king. To make matters worse, Antiochus was willing to sell the position of Kohen Gadol. Since the Second Temple was

A bust of Antiochus III (223-187 B.C.E.)

built, the ruling government had never interfered with the selection of this high office. Now, it all changed. First, a man named Jason was able to buy his way into this important job. Then, a man called Menelaus replaced him. Either way, it was bad for the Jews since neither man had deserved the job. There was another problem with Jason and Menelaus. Both men were Hellenists and not devoted Jews. They were more interested in being Greek than Jewish.

Under such Hellenist influence, it didn't take long for a gymnasium to be built in Jerusalem. There, young Jews were being tempted to play Greek games in honor of Greek gods. Altars to these gods were built all over the land. Everywhere the Jews turned, there was evidence of Greek culture. Without the leadership of a proper Kohen Gadol, and with more pagans living in their land, it became a struggle for the Jewish people to keep their belief in God and follow God's commandments.

Statue of Zeus (Jupiter) found at Caesarea. Syrian overlords forced the Jews to worship before such idols at public altars.

The Straw That Broke Their Back

Just when the people of Judea thought it couldn't get worse, it did. Antiochus decided to change the Jewish Bet HaMikdash into a temple for the Greek god Zeus. He put out the eternal flame as well as the lights of the golden menorah. He destroyed many Jewish sacred objects. Worst of all, he placed a statue of Zeus in the Temple and sacrificed pigs in front of it! Can you imagine how the people must have felt? Then Antiochus went a step farther. He made it a crime to study Torah, to keep the Sabbath, and to circumcise baby boys. Ultimately, he made it a crime, punishable by death, to be Jewish.

Being told that we can't do something often makes us want to do it more than ever. That's exactly how the Jews reacted to the laws of Antiochus. Most were determined to remain loyal to God and to Jewish beliefs. They had been treated so badly under the cruel Antiochus, they couldn't take it anymore. They were really angry! At last, they decided to fight back.

The Bully Is Paid Back

It all started in the village of Modin, northwest of Jerusalem. Syrian soldiers arrived there with new orders from the king. The Jews would now be forced to sacrifice pigs to Zeus. Mattathias, the local Jewish leader, boldly refused to obey their command. In fact, he tried to stop the Jewish people of his village from performing such a sacrifice. Instead, he and his five sons rebelled against the Syrian Greeks, killing one of them. Afterward, they fled to some caves in the nearby hillside to save their lives.

Word of the courage of Mattathias and his sons spread quickly. Soon others were also willing to be just as brave. From their hiding place, Mattathias and his family put together a small band of rebels. Antiochus and the Syrians had a fight on their hands.

The Fight Begins

In the beginning, the fighters led by Mattathias carried on simple guerrilla warfare. It must have been frustrating for the well-equipped and well-trained Syrian Greek soldiers to fight such a war. The Jews would strike quickly, and just as quickly disappear. The small band of rebels was getting the best of the large Syrian army.

An enameled picture of Judah Maccabee. It was painted in the 15th century by a French artist.

When Mattathias died, his son Judah became the leader of the revolt. Certainly you have heard of him—Judah Maccabee. His real name was Judah from the Hasmonean family. He received the nickname "Maccabee" from the battle cry his men used as they fought against Antiochus and his army. The cry was "Mi Khamokha BaElim Adonai," which translates as "Who among the gods is like God." Using just the first letter of each Hebrew word spells MKBY." The word "makabi" means "hammer" in Hebrew. Everybody thought it was a great name for Judah, who struck hammer-like blows to the enemy.

The Hammer Strikes

Judah Maccabee was an excellent general. Not only was he able to rally and inspire his troops, but he was also able to plan strategic missions. He needed both talents, because the Syrian army greatly outnumbered his little group of soldiers.

Picture what happened in the battle that took place at the Syrian encampment at Emmaus. Beforehand, Judah Maccabee may have gathered his men together to read the Torah and to pray to God. This would have reminded them that they were fighting to protect their religion. Then, Judah Maccabee revealed his clever plan. He had learned through his spies that half of the Syrian troops would be leaving to stop a rebellion in another area. He decided to surprise the half that was left behind in the military camp. As you can imagine, the remaining enemy troops were totally unprepared to defend themselves against the determined Maccabees. Judah Maccabee staged a successful attack. As an extra benefit, he also captured many of the superior Syrian weapons. When the other Syrian troops returned from a useless mission, they found their own camp in shambles. While the Maccabees celebrated, the enemy sank with defeat.

You probably know the rest. Judah Maccabee and his men soon sent the Syrians running. In 164 B.C.E., the Maccabees marched into Jerusalem. They cleaned up the Temple and destroyed the Greek idols that had been placed there. At last, the Temple was restored. Now they were ready to light the menorah once again. According to the legend, they searched and searched but could only find a small amount of oil to burn. Knowing that there was hardly enough fuel to burn for a full day, they lit the menorah anyway. It is said that a miracle happened. The little bit of oil somehow burned brightly for eight days. By then, the people were able to supply the fuel. Today we celebrate the holiday of Chanukah to remember this miracle. At the same time, we remember the Maccabees' successful fight for religious freedom.

A Greek soldier under attack. He wears a metal helmet and breastplate. This painting was found on an ancient stone coffin.

A 13th-century French manuscript, written by Benjamin the Scribe, pictures Aaron, the High Priest, pouring olive oil into the Temple menorah.

The word menorah refers specifically to the huge seven-branched golden menorah that stood in the Temple of Jerusalem.

The Torah (Exod. 25:31–40) provides the details of the Temple menorah. It was made by Bezalel and hammered out of a solid slab of gold. According to the Torah, it stood seven feet tall, weighed 100 pounds, and had seven branches.

Hasmonean Rule

It took more than 20 years for the Maccabee warriors to finally achieve their independence. Judea was free of foreign rule for the first time in hundreds of years. A group of wise leaders selected Judah Maccabee's only living brother, Simon, as Kohen Gadol, ruler and commander. Simon was the first of the Hasmonean family to lead the nation of Judea. Unfortunately, the Hasmoneans, like King Saul, were better warriors than rulers. They were not united, and they were always quarreling with one another.

To complicate matters, two very different points of view developed at this time. The two sides were called the Sadducees and the Pharisees. They weren't really political parties like the Republicans and Democrats, but they probably argued in much the same way. The Sadducees liked things the way they were and felt no need to make changes. They were mostly the wealthier Jews. They held the privileged jobs at the Temple, and many of them were successful merchants. They preferred to dress and act more like other nations because it made good business sense. Their money was used to support the Kohen Gadol, believing that he connected them to God. Their religious beliefs focused on the Temple and sacrifices. They also believed only in the Torah, which they followed to the letter of the law.

The Pharisees were a much larger group of Jews. They came from the common, everyday people. They wanted to adapt old traditions to new times. They were more flexible and accepted interpretations of the laws. They believed that the Jews should remain separate from other nations in order to keep their identity. They remembered

In Israel today Chanukah is celebrated with a relay race. A torch lit in Modin is relayed to other runners who relay the flame throughout Israel. In this way all the cities and towns become united with Modin where the story of Chanukah first began. In this photo the torch is lit and the relay race begins

the terrible influence of the Hellenists, and didn't want the same thing to happen again. Most importantly, they followed the Written Law of the Torah as well as the Oral Law, which would later become the Talmud. They believed that God had a direct connection to everyone, and could be worshiped anywhere—not just in the Temple. The experience of exile had taught them that prayer and study of God's laws were what Judaism was all about.

Eventually, the Sadducees disappeared. Their view of Judaism was just too narrow. So, when the Temple was destroyed, they were out of a job. The tradition of the Pharisees, however, lasted. The Judaism that is practiced today can be traced directly back to them. To help you remember which was which, here is a little word game. The Sadducees were the ones who disappeared, so they were "sad." The Pharisees were more flexible, so they were "fair." Does that help?

These newly discovered tombs were discovered while expanding a highway in the vicinity of Modin, ancestral home of the Maccabees. The Hebrew sign indicates that this dig is sponsored by the Israel Department of Antiquities.

There are four books of Maccabees but only two deal with the history of the Hasmonean revolt. The first book was written in Hebrew during the reign of John Hyrcanus and was translated into Greek. This passage from the Book of Maccabees was preserved in the Codex Sinaiticus, one of the great manuscripts found in the St. Catherine Monastery in Sinai.

No Unity, No Nation

The Hasmonean family feuds continued. Brother fought against brother to become the next ruler of Judea. Under such tension, the nation collapsed. The Hasmonean family had ruled an independent state for less than 80 years.

It just so happened that another strong power was waiting for the opportunity to take over Judea. The timing was perfect. While the Hasmoneans were arguing, a new conqueror arrived. Who was this great new power? What new challenges would the Jewish people have to face? Would Judaism be able to survive? A new adventure was about to unfold.

Bronze bust of Seleucus I which was found near Pompeii, Italy.

A Syrian war elephant. These huge beasts with sharp-shooting bowmen were the armored tanks of the ancient world.

YOUR JEWISH WORLD

Summarizing

In time, the people of Judea experienced a shift of power from the Egyptian Ptolemies to the Syrian Seleucids. The harsh rule of the Syrian king Antiochus angered the Jewish people. They did not appreciate his insistence that Jews make sacrifices to Greek gods. They were even angrier when he appointed Hellenist Jews to the position of Kohen Gadol. The conflict between the Judeans and Antiochus came to a head when the Temple was desecrated and Jewish practices were outlawed. Mattathias and his five sons led a revolt against these Greeks from Syria. When Mattathias died, his son Judah took control. His men, called the Maccabees, defeated the Syrian Greeks and restored the Temple. Judah Maccabee's family, the Hasmoneans, became the rulers, but they were not great leaders and fought constantly among themselves. Since the Sadducees and Pharisees had such different ideas about how to follow God, the people had trouble uniting over any issue. Another conqueror took advantage of the weakened nation.

Understanding

Did you know that after reading the Torah on Shabbat, we read the Haftarah, a portion from the books of the Prophets? It usually has an idea or message similar to the Torah portion. This practice may have originated during the rule of Antiochus, when reading of the Torah was outlawed. So, Jews studied the Prophets instead. It was such a good idea that we have continued learning from both.

Thinking

Think about how you would have resisted the Greeks. Would you have joined the Maccabees?

Investigating

Let's do something. Make a diary entry as if you were either a Maccabee or a Greek soldier at the encampment at Emmaus. Include your account of the surprise attack.

Web Resource

Go to www.ktav.com and see the **FROM UR TO ETERNITY** section

Chapter 15: The Fourth Conquerors: Forever Changed by the Romans (c. 63 B.C.E.–70 C.E.)

You learned in the last chapter that the Hasmoneans were constantly arguing among themselves. What a shame that the family could not get along. It was especially sad remembering how brave the Maccabees had been, and how much they sacrificed for their country. The Hasmoneans were so busy squabbling and competing for power that they never saw disaster coming.

So far, the Jews had outlasted the Babylonians, the Persians, and Greeks. Now they were about to face their biggest challenge of all—the Romans. Without question, the Romans were in the heavyweight division of conquerors. They were the strongest and cruelest of all. Let's find out how they changed the lives of the Jewish people.

This ancient block of stone was a part of the wall of a building in the Temple compound in Jerusalem. The Hebrew inscription reads, "To the place of trumpeting." In Temple days a priest would stand on a roof and announce by shofar blasts the approach and end of Shabbat. This inscription illustrates one of the ancient modes of communication between the priest in the Temple and the people of Jerusalem.

Powerful Pompey

The Romans came from a small town in Italy on the Tiber River, but that didn't stop them from building a huge empire. Everywhere they went, they conquered and collected countries like trophies. Nobody in the world was strong enough to defeat them. Their empire lasted about 500 years and included most of Europe, Asia, Africa, and the islands of the Mediterranean.

The Jewish people had been free for 80 years under the Hasmoneans, but freedom must not be taken for granted, as the Jews would soon discover. The year was 63 B.C.E. The Roman General Pompey was trying to win favor with the authorities in Rome by conquering as much territory as possible. Judea was an easy target. Without strong leadership to defend the tiny country, it was easy for Pompey to enter Jerusalem and force his way into the Temple. Nobody could stop him. The people must have been shocked to find a Roman general invading their holiest place.

This 15th century French painting shows Pompey and his soldiers desecrating and looting the Holy Temple.

Pompey was very curious to see what the "Jewish god" looked like. At last, he was about to discover this great mystery. When he saw no idols or images, he must have been puzzled. Perhaps he thought the people were hiding their god. As a Roman, he just couldn't understand the idea of an invisible God who is everywhere. Nevertheless, Pompey had accomplished his mission. He achieved glory for himself and Rome. He had killed 12,000 people. Jerusalem, along with all of Judea, came under Roman control. Naturally, the Romans decided to give their own name to the land they just conquered. Instead of using the Greek name, Judea, the Romans eventually called it Palestine in honor of the ancient Philistines.

Herod Who?

The Romans now set about the task of appointing leaders to rule their new territory. A man named Herod became king of Judea. Not only was he a friend of the Romans, but he was also a Jew. It seemed like a perfect combination. Herod was fortunate to have friends in high places. In fact, one of his best friends was Mark Antony, a famous Roman general. You may have heard of his wife Cleopatra. Anyway, it seemed that Herod had the right credentials. The Romans liked him, and they thought the Jews would like him, too.

Herod tried hard to win the respect of the Jewish people, but he made a big mistake. He

Herod's family tomb in Jerusalem. Here the monarch buried his wife Mariamne and his two sons after murdering them in a maniacal rage.

This is the well-preserved amphitheater in Caesarea. It was built by King Herod for the Roman governors.

decided to renovate the Temple. He thought the people would honor him for making some badly needed repairs. While he was at it, he enlarged and improved the entire structure. The result was spectacular. Stories about the beauty of Herod's Temple are legendary. Unfortunately, he didn't use his head. You see, right above the Temple gate, he placed an image of an eagle that was an emblem of the Roman Empire. Not only did this symbolize Roman control, but it also violated Jewish law against having images in the Temple. This was a double whammy for Herod. Instead of thanking him, the people became very angry.

Because Herod was sure that people didn't like him, he saw danger lurking around every corner. He was so suspicious of plots against his life that he even had members of his own family murdered. Anyone who stood in his way became a target for his revenge.

Despite his cruelty, there are some positive things for which Herod is remembered. Like Solomon, he was a great builder. He created the magnificent city of Caesaria. He built aqueducts, pipelines that carried precious water to the cities. He also constructed the fortress called Masada. This fortress was planned as his vacation spot, as well as a place for escape in case the people rebelled against him. Actually, Masada became very famous, but for a completely different reason. In the next chapter, you will learn more about Masada.

Guests in Their Own Home

Herod ruled from 37 B.C.E. to 4 B.C.E. After Herod, the Romans appointed a series of governors to run the country. It was their job to keep the peace, collect taxes, and enforce Roman law. Most of them were greedy tyrants who robbed the people. The Jews remained dependent victims of their conquerors. The burden of taxes was increasing with each new Roman governor. As the people gradually became poor, their future looked bleak.

A Difference of Opinion

All the time the governors were in power, the Jews were trying to figure out how to survive. The people didn't always agree on the best way to accomplish this. Some thought that Jews should not "make any waves." They believed it made more sense to cooperate with the much stronger Romans. They also felt that if the people stayed focused on God's laws, eventually everything would work out. There was another group, though, that didn't want to sit by and wait patiently. They were freedom fighters and rebels known as the Zealots. They urged the Jews to fight to the end—it meant they must die for God and their homeland. At first, there were very few Zealots, but just like the Maccabees, more and more supporters gradually joined them.

The "heat" was on by the time the last and worst governor, Florus, came to power. As usual, he raised taxes and stole from the Temple's treasury. The rebels were at their breaking point. By then, even more people were joining the Zealots. They wanted action!

The year was 66 C.E. Did you notice that our story of the Jews has finally taken us to the Common Era? It was 100 years after Pompey so rudely violated the Temple. The Zealots were doing what they did best. They stormed the Roman troops, and the fighting began. At first, the Zealots had some amazing victories. Fighting injus-

For five centuries, Rome dominated the ancient world. Among its conquests were, Spain, France, England, Greece and the Balkans, Mesopotamia, Armenia, Egypt, Judea, and North Africa. At its height the Roman Empire controlled an expanse which included 100 million people.
Roman armies were well equipped and led by talented commanders. Success in battle came easily to this well-disciplined fighting machine.
These Roman soldiers belonged to the Praetorian Guard, the emperor's personal bodyguards.

tice can make oppressed people very strong, but how long could they last against the huge Roman army? Over the next four years, there were many bloody battles. The Romans were not about to let this tiny country get the best of them. They beefed up their army and responded strongly to the attacks. The rebels were outnumbered about four to one. All the cities surrounding Jerusalem had surrendered, but Jerusalem itself was not giving up. The new Roman Emperor Vespasian sent his son Titus to finish the job. Titus had a foolproof plan.

A Plan for Destruction

Titus built huge mounds of dirt around the city of Jerusalem. His strategy was to trap the people inside the city's walls. If the Romans couldn't win in hand-to-hand combat, they would starve the Jews into surrender. With no way to escape, the people became weaker everyday. Eventually, Titus built ramps making it easy to wheel their heavy battering rams right up to the walls. The people were panicked when they heard the pounding and crashing, but still the city's walls stood strong. Finally, in the year 70 C.E., the Temple caught on fire. Before long, the whole city of Jerusalem was on fire. By that time, the people were exhausted and starving, and couldn't put up much resistance. A great number of people lost their lives, and many became Roman slaves. Men, women, and children were slaughtered. Their beautiful city was in ruins.

The Arch of Titus in Rome.

An Arch and a Wall

When Titus defeated the Jews, he was so excited he couldn't wait to return to Rome with his spoils of war. He carried back the seven-branched menorah, Temple treasures, and many

A copy of the carving on the Arch of Titus, showing the menorah and other objects from the Temple being paraded in triumph through the streets of Rome.

SANCTUARIES	TABERNACLE	1st. TEMPLE	2nd. TEMPLE
BUILT	c. 1280 B.C.E.	952 B.C.E.	515 B.C.E.
PLACE	SINAI DESERT	JERUSALEM	JERUSALEM
FOUNDER	MOSES	SOLOMON	ZERUBABEL
ENEMY	UNKNOWN	BABYLONIA Nebuchadnezzar	ROME Titus
DESTROYED	UNKNOWN	586-B.C.E	70 C.E.
DURATION	UNKNOWN	366 YEARS	585 YEARS

The Romans conquered Jerusalem in 70 C.E. and burned the Temple to the ground. All that remained was the Western Wall, which became a sacred place where Jews prayed. All through the centuries of exile Jews worshiped at the Western Wall. The Wall has become a place for Jews to write prayer requests and place them in the cracks between the stones.

Jewish slaves. When he arrived, he enjoyed a hero's welcome with a spectacular parade in his honor. Later, an arch was built to remember this Roman victory. The Romans were ecstatic about winning the war against the Jews. It should have been a much easier task, since they had about four times as many soldiers. Yet, it took them many years and great effort.

The Arch of Titus still stands today in the modern city of Rome. Jewish people who visit there can look up at it with pride, not shame. After all, the Roman Empire disappeared centuries ago, but we're still here!

One thing survived all of this destruction in Jerusalem. An outer retaining wall on the western side of the Temple mount was saved. You may have heard of it. It is called *HaKotel HaMa'aravi*, or the Western Wall. Actually, it was part of a wall built around the Temple area by Herod when he was king. It is the only thing left that remains from the Temple complex, the holiest site in Jerusalem. People come from all over the world to pray at the Western Wall. Someday you may have that opportunity.

THE FOUR CONQUERORS

CONQUERORS	KINGDOMS	RULERS	DATES
FIRST	BABYLON	NEBUCHADNEZZAR	721-586 B.C.E.
SECOND	PERSIA	CYRUS	538-332 B.C.E.
THIRD	GREECE	PTOLEMY	330-175 B.C.E.
FOURTH	ROME	TITUS	70 C.E.

A National Time of Mourning

Both the First and Second Temples were destroyed on the exact same date about 500 years apart. That date is Tishah B'Av, the ninth of Av. In Chapter 10, you read that the Babylonians destroyed Solomon's Temple. Now the Romans destroyed the Temple that Herod rebuilt. Jewish people everywhere still mourn on Tishah B'Av. We avoid celebrations on that day. We fast, pray, and remember both Temples. In Chapter 24, you will learn about another catastrophe that happened to our people on Tishah B'Av years later.

So, the city of Jerusalem was burned, the Temple was gone, our people were slaughtered, and those who remained were homeless. Was there any hope for the future? Could we survive? In the next chapter, you will find out what some people did to regain their freedom.

YOUR JEWISH WORLD

Summarizing

The fourth conquerors of Judea were the Romans, and they were the biggest challenge that the Jews had faced so far. The first shock came when the Roman general Pompey invaded the Temple and took possession of Jerusalem and all of the land. Then, Herod was appointed king of Judea. While he built some beautiful cities and improved the Temple, he was very cruel. The Jews hated him. After his death, a series of strict Roman governors came to power. They taxed and robbed the people. Soon, a group of rebels called Zealots began to fight back. They fought valiantly, but eventually the Temple was destroyed on Tishah B'Av, the ninth of Av, in the year 70 C.E.

Understanding

Did you know that we remember the destruction of the First and Second Temples every time there is a Jewish wedding? According to tradition, when the groom breaks the glass, we are supposed to pause from our time of joy to recall the destruction of our Temples, the first by the Babylonians, and the second by the Romans.

Thinking

Think about the Roman strategy for defeating the Jews in Jerusalem. Do you think the Jewish people could have done anything to save their city, the Temple, and themselves?

Investigating

Let's do something. Look up the Roman Empire on the Internet. Find out what a powerful nation it was over 2,000 years ago. Discover what caused it to collapse.

Web Resource

Go to www.ktav.com and see the FROM UR TO ETERNITY section

Chapter 16: Freedom Flight: The Zealots of Masada (c. 70–73 C.E.)

The situation for the Jews was bad. For the second time their beloved Temple was destroyed. It had been burned to the ground. The entire city of Jerusalem was in ruins. Thousands of Jews had been killed. They had survived three conquerors, but would they survive this devastating defeat by the Romans? Later on, we will see how the Jews were able to remain Jewish throughout their difficult history. First, though, you will meet some very unusual heroes who were so brave that they will never be forgotten.

The Jewish defenders who faced the might of Rome were poorly armed. On the other hand, the Romans were equipped with the most modern weapons of the period. Roman catapults could hurl heavy boulders with great force. The Romans also used battering rams, which destroyed defenses and paved the way for the Roman infantry.

Two Sides to Every Story

In the last chapter you learned that everybody did not react the same way to Roman terrorism. One group thought if they cooperated with the Romans, they would have a better chance of survival. They believed that you "catch more flies with honey than with vinegar." The other group, the Zealots, were rebels who believed in fighting for their cause. They were very passionate and even fought against their fellow Jews who didn't agree with them. Both groups remained devoted to God, but made different choices when faced with danger. Let's follow their exciting adventures.

The Zealots' Solution

By the time the war in Jerusalem ended, a group of Zealots had already found a great place to hide. Actually, the Romans knew where they were, but it was just difficult to get there. The hiding place was Masada, a fortress surrounded by walls high up on a plateau overlooking the Dead Sea. You learned in Chapter 15 that Herod had made Masada his special retreat. The Zealots, numbering 960 men, women, and children, went to this fortress for safety during the siege of Jerusalem.

Masada was the perfect "hiding" place. The Zealots hiked up the steep serpentine path, a winding trail on the northeast side. However, once the Romans finally decided to attack Masada, they were prevented from climbing the difficult path. The Zealots threw huge boulders and hot oil down upon them.

The fortress of Masada was built by King Herod. It has been excavated and a large part has been reconstructed.

In Jerusalem, the Romans built a mound of dirt and wood around the city to trap everyone inside. This eventually starved the people into surrender. At Masada, this strategy wouldn't work. The Jewish rebels had everything they needed for survival. They had a large food supply, and water was stored in huge cisterns, or tanks. They could grow their crops, and drink fresh rainwater. In addition, their religious needs were satisfied. They had two *mikva'ot* for ritual baths, and they even had a synagogue.

Yigael Yadin, discovered a treasure trove of artifacts which included sandals, knives, mirrors, jugs, bowls, and the greatest treasure of all - papyrus rolls containing about 40 letters from Bar Kochba.

A Shocking Discovery

For several years, the Jews were able to hold off the Roman army. Finally, General Silva, commander of the Roman troops, returned to an old successful plan of attack. They built a huge ramp to wheel their battering rams up to the fortress. Using Jewish forced labor helped make the job easier. In the year 73 C.E., the Roman troops marched up the ramp and broke through the walls of the fortress. To their astonishment, instead of hysteria and the cry of battle, they were met with complete silence. All around him, Silva saw dead bodies. Then, suddenly, seven people—two women and five children—came out of their hiding place in a cave.

These survivors told the amazing story of what had happened. They said that Eleazar ben Yair, the leader of the Zealots, saw that the end was near. He persuaded his people to take their own lives instead of submitting to Roman persecution. He warned them that the Romans would show no mercy, and the survivors would be tortured and killed. Instead, they chose death by their own hands. To prove to the Romans that this act had been their own choice, Eleazar ordered the destruction of everything except the food supply. When the Romans discovered the bodies, they would see that the Zealots had not died from starvation. This would give the rebels a moral victory. They had not allowed the Romans to capture them.

In 1963, an archaeologist named Yigael Yadin excavated Masada. He made some exciting discoveries. Among the ruins, he found some stones that were probably used to fight the Roman soldiers. He found remnants of shoes and hair, as well as 25 skeletons. There are still some unanswered questions about the people who died at Masada. Perhaps one day the answers will be found.

Today, Masada is a great tourist attraction. People are very curious about the events that occurred there almost 2,000 years ago. They want to see for themselves this incredible fortress and relive the story of the Zealots' bravery.

How Do We Know It's True?

A man named Josephus Flavius lived during this time, and was even an eyewitness to the siege of Jerusalem. Knowing this, the emperor of Rome asked him to record all the events that took place. In his book *The Jewish War*, he describes the bloody battles in Jerusalem and also tells the story of Masada. In Chapter 1 of this book, you learned that historians gather information and draw conclusions. Josephus was such an historian.

You might be interested to know that Josephus's name used to be Joseph ben Mattathias. His original name was Jewish, as he was born

Josephus before Emperor Vespasian, from a 12th century manuscript.

to Jewish parents. He even commanded Jewish forces in the north at an area called the Galilee. However, when Josephus saw that the Romans were winning, he defected to the other side. He wasn't the first person who became a traitor to save his own life, nor would he be the last. Nevertheless, we are grateful to him for his book, which reveals much about the destruction of the Temple and the flight to Masada.

Portrait coin of Vespasian, 69-79 C.E.

A More Peaceful Solution

While suicide is not accepted in Judaism, we have to understand that these were very special circumstances. The Zealots were facing certain death at the hands of the Romans. They chose suicide. There were others, however, who had different methods of dealing with the Romans. Remember the people who believed in cooperation to achieve their goal? Here is the adventure story of one very brave man who risked everything, three years before the events of Masada. He did this without fighting, but by being clever and knowing how to negotiate.

A "Deadly" Hiding Place

Yochanan ben Zakkai was a very learned man and a great scholar who lived during Roman times. When the war in Jerusalem broke out, he and his followers tried to convince the rebels that fighting was not the answer. He urged them to spend their energy keeping the faith and following God's teachings. He had a solution for Jewish survival.

Realizing that the Jews were about to lose the war, ben Zakkai devised a crafty plan that would not only save his life, but also the religion of his people. To do this, he would have to escape from Jerusalem. That would be difficult to do under the watchful eye of the Romans. Even the Zealots stopped Jews from leaving because they needed everyone's help in the fight against the Romans. So, ben Zakkai pretended to be dead. To make his death more believable, he had his students put him inside a coffin. Announcing that he died of a contagious disease, his students requested his burial outside of the city.

Once outside the city, ben Zakkai came out of the coffin. He went right up to the Roman soldiers and asked to speak with Vespasian, the Roman general. Ben Zakkai had some very exciting news for the general. He predicted that Vespasian would become the next emperor. Ben

The interior of the synagogue of Rabbi Yochanan ben Zakkai. According to tradition it was in this synagogue that Yochanan said his last prayer before being smuggled out of the besieged city of Jerusalem.

Zakkai simply reasoned that when the emperor died, Vespasian would be the most likely to be his successor. It was just common sense. Vespasian was so grateful and flattered that he agreed to grant one small favor to the Jew. All ben Zakkai wanted was to build an academy for Torah study in Yavneh, a city not far from Jerusalem. Vespasian didn't see any harm in that. If the old man wanted a school, he could have it. No big deal!

A Learning Experience

As it turned out, this school was a very big deal. It allowed the Jewish religion to remain alive in Judea even after the Temple was destroyed. Ben Zakkai had the foresight to know that scholars would have to be trained so that new leadership could be developed. These new scholars would be called Rabbis. A great tradition of learning had begun in Yavneh, and we owe it all to Yochanan ben Zakkai.

Our people were learning by experience how to survive. Before too long, we would become survival experts. You might say it was "on the job" training. Adaptation was the key to our survival. Yochanan ben Zakkai had adapted. Soon, our people would be scattered to other parts of the world. How would we face this new test of endurance without a homeland?

YOUR JEWISH WORLD

Summarizing

After the siege of Jerusalem by the Roman army, the Zealots, a group of rebels, escaped to Masada, a fortress overlooking the Dead Sea. There, they held out against the Romans for three years. As it became clear that the Roman army would storm the mountain fortress, the Zealots committed mass suicide to avoid certain death after disgrace and slavery. Yochanan ben Zakkai chose a more peaceful solution to Roman terrorism. After escaping from Jerusalem, he persuaded the Roman authorities to permit him to build a Jewish school in Yavneh. This school began a great tradition of learning and enabled Judaism to stay alive.

Understanding

Did you know that there are two references to God on the U.S. $1 bill? Check it out! The all-seeing eye, located above the pyramid, suggests divine guidance. The Latin inscription Annuit Coeptis means "God has favored our undertakings." That's a fancy way of saying that God is taking care of us.

Thinking

Think about the heroism of Yochanan ben Zakkai. What do you think would have happened to Judaism without his academy of learning?

Investigating

Let's do something. Build a model of Masada showing the Zealots in the fortress on top and the Romans below.

Web Resource

Go to www.ktav.com and see the FROM UR TO ETERNITY section

SECTION- II
WITHOUT A HOMELAND

UNIT V: A People without a Country

Chapter 17:
Skilled Survivors: The Jews Scatter (c. 73–500 C. E.)

From now on, everything would be different for the Jews. Fortunately, they had become good at adapting to new lands and new rulers. Their experiences had taught them to accept changes and make the best of them. Just think how many times their homeland had been conquered by different nations. These conquerors had come and gone, but the Jews survived despite it all. They remained a people, even as the name of their land changed. First it was called Canaan. During the reigns of Kings Saul, David, and Solomon it was named Israel. After that, it became the Divided Kingdom of Israel and Judah. The Greeks changed its name to Judea and, finally, the Romans called it Palestine. Wow! So many names for one small place!

Regardless of the name changes, most Jews didn't remain in their homeland anyway. The Romans saw to that. They scattered the Jews into distant Roman settlements. Old survival skills would be tested and new ones would be created. Let's take a look at our people from the time of the Roman conquest of Judea and beyond.

Learned Leaders

Throughout the many adventures of the Jewish people, there were always great leaders who could guide and take care of them. The newest leaders were the Rabbis, or teachers. They helped explain the laws of the Torah and they set an example of behavior for everyone to follow. Also, they were in charge of a very important Jewish political and religious institution called the Sanhedrin.

The Sanhedrin was a type of court system. Its 70 members plus its leaders made important religious and legal decisions. Their rulings were always based upon the wisdom of the Bible. Members had to know the laws of the Torah "inside and out." Obviously, only the greatest and most scholarly Rabbis qualified for membership. They met, talked, debated, and decided answers to questions about Jewish law. This court was the final authority. You might say that it was similar to the Supreme Court. With such a court in place, the Jews were able to live with one another in an orderly and peaceful way.

Head of the Sanhedrin

One of the most famous leaders of the Sanhedrin was Hillel. He lived during the beginning of the Roman rule of the Jewish homeland. In the midst of the cruelty of the Romans, Hillel was a bright light. He was kind, scholarly, and wise. His trademark was his ability to teach the lessons of the Torah with patience and love.

An engraving in a Hebrew-Latin edition of the Mishnah (1744). It illustrates a session of the Sanhedrin.

Here is a famous story about Hillel. It begins when a non-Jew came to him asking to be taught the meaning of the Torah. Showing his disrespect for a learned man, the questioner wanted Hillel to teach him everything while standing on one foot. Hillel then explained the Torah in a nutshell. He simply said, "What is hateful to you, do not do to your neighbor." If this answer sounds familiar, then you have probably heard of the Golden Rule. It says, "Love your neighbor as yourself," and comes straight out of the Torah. By using a similar statement Hillel gave a simple answer to a tricky question.

Back to Babylonia

Good leaders and an organized court system had been a great help to the Jews when they lived in a central area. However, the Jewish people were put to a real test when they settled in places away from their homeland. This "scattering" didn't take place suddenly. There were Jews living far from Jerusalem long before the destruction of the Second Temple. Of course, you remember when they were forced into Babylonia. Who could forget Nebuchadnezzar!

Let's review. After the Jews were taken to Babylonia, they were set free by the Persian king, Cyrus the Great. Only a quarter of the Jews actually returned to Jerusalem. Those who remained in Babylonia were comfortable and happy with their lives. They learned how to adapt to their new surroundings. They remained true to their belief in God with the help of prayer and the creation of gathering places, which later became synagogues. By the time the Romans destroyed the Second Temple, there was a thriving Jewish community in Babylonia.

Over time, these Babylonian Jews produced some outstanding scholars from their own academies of learning called *yeshivot*. Schools and education played an important role in maintaining Jewish life and religion. The academies in Babylonia were especially outstanding. The heads of these

These catacombs are called the Tomb of the Sanhedrin, Inside are a large number of burial chambers carved in the rock. It is the traditional place where the members of the Sanhedrin were buried. The tomb is in Jerusalem.

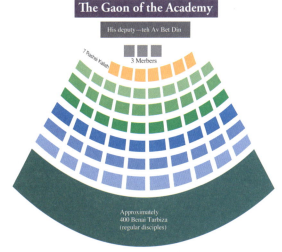

The Talmudic Academies in Babylonia were headed by a gaon. It consisted of 70 sages whose places in the hierarchy were fixed. The sages closer to the gaon, were generally the more learned.

schools were great men known as the Ge'onim. It was their job to answer all the questions about Jewish laws. The answers to these questions are called responsa. Of course, some of these questions may have come from Jews living far away. Don't forget that it was hard for many people to travel in those days, and there were no telephones or internet. So, letters were carried by special messengers who traveled by boat, foot, or camel. This system was slow but it worked.

Mishnah Accomplished

Meanwhile, the Jews were constantly in need of scholarly explanations of the Torah and its laws. Usually the answers to questions on Jewish law were passed from one person to another by word of mouth. These discussions became known as the Oral Law. It was full of wisdom, but very few could possibly remember all of it. Something had to be done.

One famous Jewish scholar, Rabbi Akiva (c.50-135 C.E.) went into action. He devised a way of organizing and categorizing the Oral Law so that it was easier to remember and follow. What he didn't do was write it down. That would happen shortly after his death.

The scholar Judah ha Nasi (c. 135-220 C.E.) was born the same year that Rabbi Akiva died. He dedicated his whole life to finishing the job of preserving the Oral Law. It was hard work, but he and his students did it. This time everything was written down and became known as the Mishnah.

A page from Mishnah Ketubot. The Mishnah is in the center. To the right is the commenatry of Rashi. To the left are the commentaries of Baalei Hatosefot.

More in the Gemara

For a few hundred years Jewish scholars in both Jerusalem and Babylonia studied the Mishnah. They wrote down their comments about it. These commentaries were called the Gemara. The Mishnah helped explain the Torah, and the Gemara helped explain the Mishnah. At last there would be a permanent record of the Oral Law. The Mishnah together with the Gemara is known as the Talmud. We can also call the Talmud, the Oral Law written down.

One version of the Talmud was completed in Jerusalem about 425 C.E., and another in Babylonia about 500 C.E. Since the greatest scholars were in Babylonia, the Babylonian Talmud is considered the higher authority. The Torah and the Talmud form the foundation of Judaism.

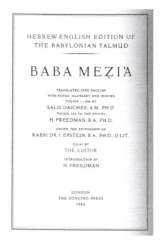

Several editions of the Talmud have been translated into English. This is one of the title pages of the Soncino edition, published in England.
In 1923 Rabbi Meir Shapiro decided to create a course of Talmud study which he called Daf Yomi. The word daf means "page" and yomi means "daily." Rabbi Shapiro's plan was to study all 2711 pages (dapim) of the Talmud in seven and a quarter years. Today, many people all over the world participate in the Daf Yomi program. Some study the Talmud individually, some in groups which use both the original and the English translation. There are Daf Yomi groups in Hollywood, the Senate in Washington, and the boardroom of Wall Street.

New Horizons in the Diaspora

It was a good thing that the Jewish people had so many tools to keep their religious beliefs alive. They were going to need them all—schools, prayer, synagogues, Torah, and Talmud. You see, it would take another 2,000 years after the Roman conquest before they would again control their homeland and call it Israel. During the years in between, Jews spread to lands all over the world. They lived under the rule of other nations, sometimes in harmony and sometimes in hostility. This worldwide scattering of the Jews is known as the Diaspora. This includes us. Anyone living outside of Israel is in the Diaspora.

It's not difficult to understand how Jews arrived in so many places. They were simply looking for a better life. When one society treated them badly, they moved on to another. The first Diaspora was in Babylonia, where Jews remained and thrived for hundreds of years. Later, the Diaspora covered the world. All the while, a few Jews stayed in and around Jerusalem and other parts of their homeland.

Wherever they went, the Jews left their mark. Their devotion to God and care for one another was always noticed. At the same time, they were exposed to, and influenced by, other people. Most of the time, the Jews could borrow the good traits of others and discard what they didn't like. Their situation became most dangerous when other religions began to grow and strengthen. Unfortunately, the leaders of these religions were not always tolerant of the Jews. What were these new religions? How did they begin? You will learn about them next.

YOUR JEWISH WORLD

Summarizing

As you can see, Jews are survivors. The Roman conquest really put them to the test. With the support of great institutions like the Sanhedrin, and great scholars like Hillel, the Jewish people were strengthened. They also gained a lot from the thriving community in Babylonia. Another important development was the creation of the Talmud, the Oral Law written down. All of this prepared them for the Diaspora. From Roman times on, the Jews would be scattered throughout the world.

Understanding

Did you know that Hillel, who lived 2,000 years ago, made decisions that affect you even today? Have you ever wondered why you light one Chanukah candle the first night, two on the second, and so on, until all eight are burning? (No, it's not so you can get eight presents.) It's because Hillel thought it would be a good idea to increase the light of the miracle each night.

Thinking

Think about how hard it would be to understand the Torah without the explanations of the Talmud. Do you use any other books that require an explanation to make them clear?

Investigating

Let's do something. Find a copy of the Talmud at your synagogue or in a library. Notice how the pages are traditionally laid out, and how many commentaries there are for each passage.

Web Resource

Go to www.ktav.com and see the
FROM UR TO ETERNITY section

Chapter 18: Two New Religions Enter the Scene: Christianity and Islam (c. 1–700 C.E.)

Did you know that Judaism influenced the development of two other important religions? These religions are Christianity and Islam. Did you know that each of these religions has had a huge impact on the Jewish people? Actually, the next several hundred years of Jewish history have a lot to do with surviving the power of these two religious groups. That's because most of our people eventually lived in lands controlled by the followers of Christianity or Islam. For that reason, you will probably want to learn a little something about how each got started. You might also be curious to learn about your friends and neighbors who don't share your religious beliefs.

Waiting for the Messiah

Before learning about Christianity we must return for a moment to Roman times. During the Roman Conquest, the Jewish people lived in constant fear. The Romans were often cruel and had little regard for human life. Their entertainment was watching gladiators, men who fought to their death against wild beasts. They took people from their homes and sold them into slavery. So, it's not surprising that the Jewish people were eager for the Messiah to come right away, to deliver them from turmoil. Judaism teaches that when the Messiah comes Jews from all over the world will gather together in Israel and there will be peace everywhere. In difficult times, people especially long for this to happen. By the way, the word Messiah means the "anointed." In biblical times kings were anointed or crowned by sprinkling special oil on their heads. Jews believe that the Messiah will come from the family of King David.

From time to time men appeared claiming to be the Messiah. Some of these men attracted followers. The most famous was a Jew named Yeshua. Now we call him Jesus. That's right! Jesus was born a Jew. He taught his small group of followers to believe in God and to be good and kind. His followers were so impressed with his teachings that they believed he was the son of God, chosen to be the Messiah. Most Jews could not accept Jesus as the Messiah because he did not meet the requirements for such a claim. After all, the world was certainly not at peace. So, they didn't pay much attention to him.

However, the Romans did notice Jesus. Because he was preaching his beliefs all over the land, they were afraid he would become too powerful and stir up trouble. To stop him, the Romans had him put to death.

Christianity Is Created

Often, leaders become even more powerful after they die a brave, violent death. Sometimes, things get blown out of proportion. The memory of these leaders becomes so sweet, it begins to take on a life of its own. That is exactly what happened in this case. Jesus became even

The ruins of the ancient synagogue of Kfar Nahum (Capernaum) on the northwest shore of the Sea of Galilee. According to Christian belief, Jesus visited and preached in this synagogue.

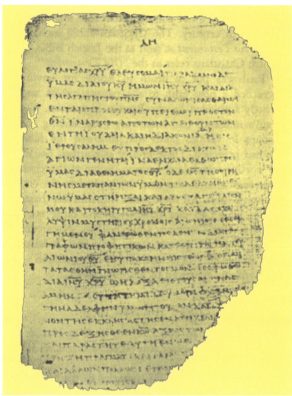

Earliest known manuscript of the letters of Paul, 200 C.E.

more important after he died. That happened due to a man named Paul.

Paul taught that Jesus was the Son of God and the Messiah. Paul traveled to countries far and wide preaching this message. He made Jesus famous. Judaism teaches that we are all children of God, so the notion that one human being was superior or divine was impossible for the Jews to accept. But Paul continued his journey, gaining supporters along the way. He became a missionary, someone who spreads ideas. Eventually, those ideas became a completely new religion. By now you have probably guessed that this new religion was Christianity.

Gradually, Christianity grew in importance as more people became believers. As time went on, the religion got a real boost from an unlikely source—the Romans. It seems that Christianity grew very popular in Rome. Many Roman leaders converted to Christianity, and eventually it became the official religion of the Empire. At the same time, the Roman Empire was getting stronger and stronger. Rome was taking over the European continent. With the Romans came Christianity. That's how most of Europe became Christian. Isn't it strange that the same empire that killed Jesus later became Christian? Today the Roman Empire is a thing of the past, but Christianity has survived for more than 2,000 years. Don't forget that Judaism is almost 2,000 years older than that.

Muhammad and Islam

Now let's meet the man who started the religion of Islam. It all began about 600 years after Jesus, in the city of Mecca, which is in the country we now call Saudi Arabia. In those days, it was just called Arabia. This was the birthplace of Muhammad, the founder of Islam. Here is his story.

Muhammad grew up as a poor, orphaned, camel driver. Luckily for him, he started working for a very wealthy older woman. They fell in love, married, and lived a happy life together. Being a camel driver was a great job for him because he got to see the world and travel to faraway places. In his travels, he met many Jews and Christians. He was especially fascinated with their belief in one God. You see, his people were idol worshipers. This bothered him a great deal.

An old painting showing Muhammad preaching to the non-believers.

This 16th century Turkish painting shows an angry mob of the citizens of Mecca throwing stones at Muhammad. Because of their hostility he was forced to flee the city, but eight years later he returned in triumph. Note the halo around Muhammad's featureless face.

Soon, he would try to convince his people—the Arabs—to give up their pagan ways.

One day, while deep in thought, Muhammad had a dream. In this dream, the angel Gabriel told him that he was to become a messenger of God. Muhammad had many dreams after that. He was certain that God was speaking with him. Years later, the content of these dreams was recorded in a book called the Koran. Muhammad believed that he was special. He declared that he was the greatest and final prophet of all.

Muhammad was now ready to start a new career—converting people to his new religion, Islam. He started preaching in his hometown of Mecca. He wanted everyone to forget their idols and start believing in Allah (Arabic for God). It saddened him that only a few would listen. He became such a bother to the residents of Mecca that some plotted his murder. Muhammad had no choice. He and his few followers fled to a neighboring city, Medina.

View of the holy city of Mecca and its mosque. Muhammadan pilgrims come from great distances to a black stone called the kaaba which is enclosed in the square shelter in the middle of the mosque court. Muhammad claimed that the kaaba was sanctified by Abraham and Ishmael.

First Medina, Then the World

Muhammad thought he would have better luck in Medina, where there were lots of Jews. He believed the monotheistic Jews would accept his teachings. He was mistaken. The Jews would not buy into it. As it happened, the Christians didn't accept his teachings either. However, he was successful in converting many of the pagans. Some of them were wealthy and important citizens. Eventually, he had enough power to begin a war with Mecca. He wanted to teach his enemies a lesson they would never forget.

When his army defeated the people of Mecca, Muhammad became an instant hero. This victory made it easy for him to gain more converts to Islam. The followers of Islam are called Muslims. With his new strength and large following, Muhammad now turned against the Jews. He could never forgive their rejection, and he killed many of them on the spot. Jewish life in that part of the world would never again be the same.

It did not take long for Muhammad and his growing military power to conquer most of Arabia. Even after he died, his followers continued to defeat other nations, converting them to Islam. Encouraged by their success in their own part of the world, they began to branch out into other regions. First, they spread their power to what was once the Persian Empire, and then they turned toward Northern Africa. They were finally stopped in Spain. The Muslims had won a vast area of land roughly bordered by the Mediterranean Sea. What a mighty force they must have been!

An ancient painting showing Muhammad with the leader of a Jewish tribe in Arabia. He condemned the whole tribe to death because they refused to convert to the Muslim religion.

THREE RELIGIONS

FOUNDER	ABRAHAM	JESUS	MUHAMMAD
RELIGIONS	JUDAISM	CHRISTIANITY	ISLAM
DATES	c. 1900 B.C.E.	65 C.E.	622 C.E.
TIME LAPSE		1965 YEARS	557 YEARS

Jews (wearing their traditional colored costumes) consult a 120-year-old elder in Damascus, who tells them that Muhammad was a Messiah and the last prophet to come into the world. In this period there were constant discussions about the roles of the three religions- Judaism, Christianity, and Islam. This is a 16th century Turkish miniature based on a 10th century Arab text.

In a Nutshell

Now you know a little about the birth of two great religions. Both Christianity and Islam were richly influenced by Jewish beliefs. Both are based on monotheism, the belief in one God. Both were started by men who believed they had a special connection to God. Finally, both religions wanted the acceptance of the Jews but were unsuccessful. Despite these similarities, the Christians and Muslims were vastly different from each other and from the Jews. Today, these two religions are practiced all over the world. However, long ago, Europe was mostly Christian, and Northern Africa and the Middle East was mostly Muslim. Soon you will meet Jews who lived in lands controlled by each of these religions.

YOUR JEWISH WORLD

Summarizing

Judaism had a great influence on the formation of two other religions. Christianity began with a Jew named Jesus. His followers believed that he was the son of God. After the Romans killed Jesus, Paul spread Jesus's teachings and gained a large following. In time, most of the Roman Empire and most of Europe accepted Christianity.

A man by the name of Muhammad was the founder of Islam. He claimed to be a prophet of God. Following several military victories, Muhammad was able to spread his religious beliefs throughout Arabia. The Muslims' military power continued even after Muhammad's death. With one victory after another, Islam soon controlled Northern Africa, the Middle East and Spain.

Understanding

Did you know that a tool called Jacob's Staff, which measured the position of the sun, made it possible for navigators to know the location of their ships at sea? This tool was invented by Levi ben Gershom, a Jew, and was used by Christopher Columbus, on his voyage of discovery.

Thinking

Think about all the ways Judaism has influenced the world.

Investigating

Let's do something. Draw the emblems of Judaism, Christianity, and Islam.

Web Resource

Go to www.ktav.com and see the FROM UR TO ETERNITY section

Chapter 19: Different Paths: Ashkenazim and Sephardim

Surely, you are now getting the message that our people have had many disappointments in their struggle for survival. Just when one hurdle was crossed, another would appear. The two new religions, Christianity and Islam, certainly added to these difficulties. Each one claimed to have the "true" answers and left no room for differences of opinion. Centuries ago terrible wars were fought because of religion. Jews were usually targets of abuse because they refused to abandon their Covenant with God. Unfortunately, people are still fighting over religion. Religious wars continue today in the same way they did hundreds of years ago. Isn't it too bad that we haven't learned from the past?

Painting by Hieronymus Hess, in the art museum of Basel, Switzerland. The Jews were forced to attend conversion sermons by Catholic priests. Note the priest slapping a Jew for snickering or for falling asleep.

Let's Face Reality

From the Roman conquest on, Jews would not be living in their own land. Instead, they would be living in lands that were controlled by others. We could only yearn for the wonderful kingdoms of Saul, David, and Solomon. We would just have to keep plugging away and try to adjust to living without a homeland for a long time to come.

To survive, we would need to learn to live as Jews surrounded by the new and strong religious beliefs of Christianity and Islam. Those Jews who settled in countries in Europe, such as France and Germany, were under Christian control. Those who lived around the Mediterranean Sea in countries such as Spain, Morocco, Egypt, Turkey, and Syria were under Muslim control.

Two of a Kind

Life was very different for the Jews who lived with the Christians compared to those who lived with the Muslims. It makes sense if you think about it. Most of Christian Europe has a cooler climate than the Muslim area around the Mediterranean Sea. Because of this they don't share the same customs and lifestyle. It will help you understand this by contrasting different regions of your own country. For example, in the United States, the climate and geography vary from state to state. In January a girl living in

ASHKENAZIM-SEPHARDIM			
PEOPLE	LANGUAGE	AREA	ROOTS
ASHKENAZIM	YIDDISH	EUROPE	GERMAN
SEPHARDIM	LADINO	MEDITERRANEAN ASIA	ARABIC SPANISH

Florida might swim in the ocean, while a boy in Colorado might ski in the mountains.

Now you can see why the result of living in two different regions produced two groups of Jews. These groups had their own way of dressing, their own special foods, and their own Jewish traditions. They even had their own way of pronouncing Hebrew. We have two names for them. One group is called Ashkenazim, the other Sephardim.

The Ashkenazim were Jews who lived among the Christians in Eastern and Central Europe. Askenazim means German in Hebrew. As you might expect most of their ancestors once lived in Germany. They spoke Yiddish, a mixture of German and Hebrew.

The Jews who lived among the Muslims in Spain, Portugal, Northern Africa, and the Middle East were called Sephardim. The word Sepharad is Hebrew for Spain. You probably figured out that many of the Sephardim can trace their ancestry to Spain. These Jews spoke Ladino, a mixture of Spanish and Hebrew.

There are Ashkenazim and Sephardim today. The differences are only in their traditions but not in their religion. That remains the same. They are all Jewish. By the way you may be able to trace your own ancestors back to one of these groups. You may have to do some digging because now Ashkenazim and Sephardim are all mixed together.

Sink or Swim

It took a lot of strength, courage, and determination for the Jewish people to survive without a homeland. The Diaspora was certainly making things more difficult. We were now forced to live in many other lands. It would have been much easier to just give up. After all, other nations had disappeared when faced with similar difficulties. Think about it. Our old enemies from King David's time, the Philistines, Edomites, and

David Sassoon and three of his sons c. 1850. David Sassoon understood that the Muslims would never allow the Jews to live in peace, so he moved his family and his business. The Sassoon family, were Sephardim from Baghdad, who relocated to Bombay, India. They were called the "Rothschilds of the East." They directed an enormous commercial empire which included factories, financial institutions, and trading companies in all major Far Eastern countries.

Moabites, were long gone. It is as if they melted away. The Babylonians, Persians, and Greeks lost their territories and no longer remained a separate people. They simply blended into the nations, which had conquered them. Even the mighty Romans are no longer around today. Yet, here we are—Jews. We have outlasted them all!

The Jewish Secret to Survival

By this time, you probably have your own ideas about how the Jewish people have survived so many hardships. Maybe you have noticed some patterns of behavior. They are the tools we developed in order to survive. Let's talk about them.

One key tool was our strong belief in God and the Covenant we shared. Abraham made an agreement with God about 4,000 years ago, and this agreement *(Brit)* still binds us today. The Jewish people promised to believe in God, and God promised to watch over the Jewish people. To this day we feel that we are protected by this special arrangement.

We also survived because we knew when to make changes. Do you remember what happened when Nebuchadnezzar destroyed our first Temple? When we no longer had a specific place to worship, we came up with a great idea to gather in meeting places, which were later called synagogues. That way, even without a Temple, we could be Jewish anywhere.

We began to realize that we could adapt yet still remain Jewish. This lesson became quite clear when the Greeks ruled us. It would have been very easy to have become Hellenists and follow Greek ways. Most of us didn't. We learned that we could admire Greek scholarship, and accept some new ideas without giving up our religious beliefs. To put it quite simply, we learned to gain from others without being totally changed by them.

No matter where we lived, we continued to study our religion. Education was always important. You saw just how important it was in Chapter 16. When Yochanan ben Zakkai was granted only one wish, he asked for a school to be built in Yavneh. The lessons we learn from the Torah and Talmud continue to teach us how to be good Jews and how to make the world a better place.

Simply Surviving

It wasn't easy for our people to survive within so many different cultures, but we did. In the next chapters, you will see all the pressures we had to endure. We bent a little, but did not break. We learned to live with the Babylonians, the Persians, the Greeks, and the Romans. For hundreds of years to come, we would need to live with the Christians and the Muslims. You won't be surprised to learn that even harder times were ahead.

The Ashkenazim and Sephardim experienced many adventures in their new lands. Some were good and others bad. One thing was certain. Our people developed great skills that allowed them to survive and flourish.

YOUR JEWISH WORLD

Summarizing

After the Roman conquest, the Jewish people scattered to many other lands. Most of our people lived in lands controlled by either Christians or Muslims. The Jews who lived in Europe in countries such as France or Germany were under Christian control. They became known as Ashkenazim. Those Jews who lived along the Mediterranean Sea in countries such as Turkey, Spain, or Egypt were under Muslim control. They became known as Sephardim. Because they lived in different regions of the world, the Ashkenazim and Sephardim had different customs. In both regions our people had to face many hardships and develop many ways to survive. We learned how to live with others while still holding strong to Judaism. These skills would be very important to us as we faced new challenges.

Understanding

Did you know that Sephardic Jews name their babies after living relatives? Ashkenazic Jews almost never do that. They name their babies after relatives who have passed away.

Thinking

Think about all the ways the Jewish people have survived throughout the ages. What keeps us strong today?

Investigating

Let's do something. Find out if your ancestors were Ashkenazim or Sephardim. Ask family members to share some of their traditions.

Web Resource

Go to www.ktav.com and see the FROM UR TO ETERNITY section

UNIT VI: Jewish Survival in Europe
Chapter 20: No Castles for Jews: Daily Life (c. 700–1096 C.E.)

We are now ready to follow the adventures of our people as they lived in Christian lands. In this chapter we will meet the Ashkenazim who lived in the countries we now call England, France, Germany, Hungary, and Poland—to name just a few. Life was uneasy for them. That's because they never knew where they stood with their Christian neighbors. At times they were welcomed, and at other times they were treated as despised intruders. Settlements were started, then abandoned, then started somewhere else. Let's go back and figure out just how the Jews came to live in these areas.

Stepping Back

It all began when the Romans destroyed the Second Temple in 70 C.E. You remember when the Jewish people were without a Temple and without a land to call their own. They were scattered throughout the Roman Empire—throughout the Diaspora. They tended to settle in cities and places with a lot of trading and business. Many went to the areas that would become France and Germany. As time went by, Jewish communities sprang up all over Europe.

Trouble Ahead

While the Jews were finding new places to live, Christianity was growing. Before long, Christians greatly outnumbered Jews. They constantly pressured the Jews to convert. Because the Church controlled the governments, laws were passed that made Jewish life difficult. Yet, even with this hardship, Judaism continued to survive.

Let's take a look at some of those laws that were aimed against Jews. One law prohibited the marriage of a Christian and a Jew. Another law prohibited Jews from holding public office. From time to time, rules were passed that

Jews were required by law to wear pointed hats and yellow badges.

The old town hall in the Jewish ghetto in Prague. Throughout Europe, the Jews were gradually herded into ghettos as the Middle Ages progressed, the first compulsory ones being established in Venice in 1516. The Christian argument was that faith would be weakened by the presence of Jews, who, outside the ghettos, were forced to wear identification badges.

forbade the construction of synagogues. Worst of all, Jewish children were sometimes taken away from their parents and forced to be educated as Christians. For whatever reason, Jews were often seen as a threat, and were therefore persecuted, belittled, and shamed.

A Jewish Genius

It seems almost impossible, but Jewish culture continued to grow and develop even under such difficult circumstances. In fact, one of the greatest Ashkenazic scholars was born in France in 1040. His name was Rabbi Shlomo ben Yitzchak, known as Rashi. If you look carefully at his given name you can figure out how he got his nickname. Like many Jews of this time, he probably owned vineyards and produced wine to support his family. In addition to this business, Rashi operated a famous school for Jewish studies.

To this day, the teachings of Rashi are valuable and widely quoted. Many of our Jewish books include his comments and written discussions. He was able to explain the Jewish Bible and the Talmud in a very clear and orderly way. Rashi had the amazing ability to use stories and tales to make his point. That's why his ideas were so easy to understand. No wonder we still study his works 1,000 years later.

Rashi had three children, all daughters. In those days it was quite unusual for girls to be educated, but Rashi encouraged them in their studies. They, too, became brilliant Jewish scholars. His daughters married men who were also intelligent and scholarly. Even Rashi's grandchildren followed in the family tradition. It just proves that "the apple doesn't fall far from the tree." These family members continued Rashi's great academy of Jewish studies long after he died. They also wrote many additions *(Tosafot)* to his works. Together his followers are referred to as the Tosafists.

The Rashi chapel in the city of Worms, the synagogue where the great commentator worshiped and taught.

Reading and Writing

Rashi's school was not the only one in Europe. Wherever Jews lived, they created schools for their children. Some were large academies with lots of students. Others were simply a one-room school *(cheder)* where a child could learn to read, write, and study the Torah. In those days, it was unusual for an ordinary person to be literate. Except for royalty, most Christians never attended school and didn't know how to read or write. The Jews were different; as they valued education very highly.

Education had its advantages and disadvantages for the Jews. It was an advantage because some kings invited Jewish people to live in their cities. They believed that wherever Jews went, the economy flourished. They believed that educated Jews would make important contributions to their kingdoms. These kings promised to protect their Jewish subjects. Of course, if the king changed his mind or a new ruler took over, the future once again became uncertain. Education was also a disadvantage, because it made the Jews unpopular. Their Christian neighbors were jealous of their knowledge and the special treatment they received from the king.

Sails and Sales

Wherever they lived, most Jews had to struggle to keep their families clothed, fed, and housed. Not all occupations were open to them. However, there was one way many Jews did make a living. They became merchants. These merchants established Jewish communities all over Europe. In turn, the merchants prospered because of these communities. It was a good arrangement.

Here's how it worked. It was necessary for a merchant to do a lot of traveling. He would buy goods in one place and sell them in another. Communities relied upon the tradesman to bring them goods that were not readily available in their own area. The life of a merchant was filled with constant travel and much danger. Wherever he went, the Jewish merchant looked for other Jews. He knew that he would be safe in a Jewish home, and he would be able to communicate in their common language of Hebrew. Also, he could trust his fellow Jews in matters of credit and loans.

The traveling merchant was often a good source of news. He brought reports of events and family matters from one community to the next. The local Jews, happy to receive such news, eagerly welcomed the merchant into their synagogues and homes. Over time some merchants set up trading posts in faraway places. These often became the seeds for new Jewish colonies.

As time went on, some Jews joined great explorers and adventurers. They helped to navigate and prepared the course of travel. Jewish astronomers and navigators, both Ashkenazim and Sephardim, invented several instruments used to help sailors find their way on the high seas. In addition, Jewish mapmakers provided another important service for travelers. As usual, Jews were making great contributions to the world.

Jews played a significant role in the lively cultural life of Christian Spain. Their knowledge of languages, and close acquaintance with Muslim customs and intellectual tradition became quite helpful. In the picture is a map depicting the Jewish silktraders' route. The map was devised by the Castilian Jewish cartographer Abraham Cresques (died in 1387) and his son Judah for the Crown Prince Don Juan.

An astrolabe with Jewish writing constructed by a Jewish astronomer for Alfonso the Wise, king of Castile.

Engraving of a Jewish moneylender, Augsburg, Germany, 1531.

As you can see, Ashkenazim led a very complicated life. They were never sure when the townspeople would approve of them or scorn them. If they were successful in business, their neighbors were jealous. If they were struggling to get by, only fellow Jews would help. On top of all this, there was the ongoing pressure to become Christian. Most Christians simply couldn't understand why Jews remained Jews—no matter how tough it was made for them. Can you imagine how difficult it must have been to be Jewish? As you read on, you will discover more challenges that our people faced in Europe.

Money Matters

In some places Jews were prohibited from the most common ways of making a living. For example, they could not be farmers because they weren't allowed to own land. They were often banned from learning trades and crafts. However, Jews were allowed to be bankers and moneylenders, which Christians refused to do. These professions were not considered to be proper for Christians. Educated Jews, on the other hand, knew how to keep records and deal with money. They were perfect for the job.

Most cities and villages needed someone to take care of financial matters. The Jewish moneylender could help a person in need of funds to start a new business, buy equipment, or pay off a debt. Yet, the Jews were hated for the control they had over money. They were resented for the interest they charged on loans. It all seems matter-of-fact today, but back then "modern" business practices were met with disgust. To be sure, it was a "no win" situation for the banker. The unfortunate moneylender was seen as suspicious. The Christians thought they were being cheated no matter how honest the Jewish lender might be.

Mayer Amschel Rothschild's birthplace in the Frankfurt ghetto. He laid the foundations of his family's fortunes through his skillful handling of Elector William I's investments. His sons set up banking houses in London, Paris, Vienna, and Naples.

THE RASHI SCRIPT

Mem Sofit	ם	ם	Alef	א	ֿא
Nun	נ	ב	Beit	ב	ב
Nun Sofit	ן	ן	Gimel	ג	ג
Samech	ס	ס	Daled	ד	ד
Ayin	ע	ט	Hay	ה	ה
Fay	פ	פ	Vav	ו	ו
Fay Sofit	ף	ף	Zayin	ז	ז
Tzadi	צ	ל	Chet	ח	ח
Tzadi Sofit	ץ	ץ	Tet	ט	ט
Quf	ק	ק	Yud	י	י
Resh	ר	ר	Khaf	כ	כ
Sin	ש	ש	Khaf Sofit	ך	ך
Tav	ת	ת	Lamed	ל	ל

Rashi was a prolific scholar and was constantly writing new commentaries. It was difficult and very time-consuming to write using the regular Hebrew alefbet. So Rashi used a cursive script that was much easier and faster to write.

Most of the early commentaries on the Torah and the Talmud were printed in Rashi script.

YOUR JEWISH WORLD

Summarizing

After the Roman conquest, Jews settled throughout the Roman Empire. Over the course of several hundred years, Jewish communities became dispersed all over the European continent. In the meantime, Jewish learning never stopped. Academies of Jewish study sprang up throughout Europe, particularly in France and Germany. The great scholar Rashi started one such academy. Because of their emphasis on education, Jewish people were mostly literate and knowledgeable, while others were mostly illiterate and unschooled. In addition, their education made Jews sought after by some kings and gave them opportunities to become successful businesspersons. During this time, many Jews worked as merchants and moneylenders.

Understanding

Did you know that the British were responsible for creating the jury system? A thousand years ago, the Jews of England persuaded the king to agree to settle certain disputes between Jews and Christians using a jury of 12 people. But where did they get that idea? It came from the Sanhedrin.

Thinking

Think about the life of a traveling Jewish merchant over 1,000 years ago. In what ways did being Jewish make the journeys easier? In what ways harder?

Investigating

Let's do something. Find a copy of Rashi's commentaries. Notice the different script, or style of writing, that is used. Try writing in Rashi script.

Web Resource

Go to www.ktav.com and see the FROM UR TO ETERNITY section

Chapter 21: More Trouble: The Persecutions Continue (c. 1096–1500 C.E.)

About 1,000 years ago, things reached the boiling point with the Christians. This time it was the Muslims, not the Jews, who were the main targets of their anger. The Christians wanted to kick the Muslims out of the Holy Land, Israel, which was also Jesus's birthplace. To do this, they organized a holy war. Knights in shining armor were recruited to fight for the honor of their religion. Thousands of men came forward to answer this appealing call to become soldiers for Christianity. They were called Crusaders. They began their march toward Jerusalem from all over Europe. These Crusades changed the lives of all Europeans.

Knights were intolerant of other religions. They fought passionately and ruthlessly for Christianity.
Note the Christian cross on their clothing and shields.

Knights Cause Nightmares

So what did this have to do with the Jews? The Crusaders' religious passion made them extremely intolerant of all non-Christians. As you might guess, the innocent Jews who happened to live in their path suffered greatly. Many were murdered. Some were given the horrible choice of converting to Christianity or being killed. One wave after another of Crusaders marched through Europe. They believed they were acting as good Christians, yet they slaughtered many people along the way. For approximately 200 years, beginning with the First Crusade in 1096, these knights and their followers left a trail of death and devastation.

After the Crusades, the Jewish communities of Europe were never the same. The Ashkenazim felt insecure. They knew that such unprovoked violence could happen again. Their Christian neighbors had also changed. They began to accuse the Jews of all sorts of unreasonable offenses. Rumors were flying, which caused hostility toward the Jews.

In 1475 the city of Trent, in northern Italy, was the scene of blood libel near a home in a Jewish community. After questioning under torture, 17 Jews confessed and were condemned to death. Jews were not allowed to live in Trent until the 18th century.
Gandolfino d' Asti, Martyrdom of Simon of Trent. Oil, late 15th century.

Bloody Gossip

Have you ever had a lie told about you? Think how terrible it would be if everyone believed it no matter how hard you tried to set matters straight. Consider how bad it would be to have it spread and grow more powerful. Well, this is what happened to the Jews of Europe.

It all started in England during the holiday of Passover in 1144. The body of a boy was found not far from the home of a Jew. Someone falsely blamed Jews for killing the boy. To make matters worse they claimed that the boy was killed so that his blood could be used to make matzah. How ridiculous! Our religion condemns murder, and obviously never demands that we kill children. What's more, it is forbidden for Jews to drink blood. The guidelines for keeping kosher teach us to remove as much blood from our meat as possible. Nevertheless, this terrible untruth about their "alien" neighbors spread like wildfire all over Europe. These kinds of false accusations came to be called the Blood Libel. It was just another excuse to persecute the Jews.

Edict of Louis VI banishing the Jews from France in 1145. He stole their homes, money, and personal property. By exiling the Jews he cancelled his large debt to the Jewish moneylenders. The clever king also collected all the debts owed to the Jews by his Christian subjects.

Thrown Out Again

About 150 years after the Blood Libel rumors began, the Jews of England were ordered to leave the country. In other words, they were expelled from the land. As a matter of fact, Jews were forced out of many European countries. Usually, the king would tax the Jews very heavily. When they no longer had any money, the king would issue an order for expulsion. The Jews had no choice. They would move to another country until they were again forced to leave. The Jews were not entirely accepted or at home anywhere for very long. Because they were unwanted in Western Europe, the Jews gradually moved in large numbers to Eastern Europe. The Jewish population increased in countries such as Poland and Lithuania, where rulers welcomed them. In time, the majority of Ashkenazim lived in Eastern Europe.

In 1242 the French king Louis the Ninth ordered that the books of the Talmud were to be assembled and burned. Pictured above is the burning of the books of the Talmud in Paris, France.

Dressing for the Part

Even if the Jewish people wanted to blend in with their neighbors, they were not allowed to do so. They were required to put on certain clothes that would immediately identify them as Jews. In some areas they were forced to wear tall pointed hats. In other places they had to wear a yellow badge on their clothing. This requirement was also a way to get money from the Jews, because the hats and badges had to be purchased at extremely high prices. No matter what they were ordered to wear, the effect was the same—it was easy for everyone to spot a Jew.

Rats and Fleas

In the year 1348, a terrible illness spread throughout Europe. Back then, it was called the Black Death, but today we know it as the bubonic plague. The disease was caused by the bite of fleas carried on rats. About one-third of the people living in Europe died from the plague. As you can imagine, everyone was frightened. Some turned to religion, which meant a renewed interest in Christianity. Others became angry. Neither of these reactions was good for the Jews.

With the disease raging, and the inability to stop it, Europeans began blaming "the Jews" for causing the illness. They were certain that people were dying because the city water supplies had been poisoned. They were equally certain that the Jews were responsible. In a time when most people were uneducated, it seemed to be a perfectly reasonable explanation for such a plague, especially since they noticed that fewer Jews became sick. The people didn't realize that Jews washed their hands before eating and observed the cleanliness of keeping kosher. Jews also bathed more regularly and scrubbed their houses for Shabbat. These religious practices gave some protection to the Jews. Nevertheless, in their confusion, anger, and religious rage, the Europeans needlessly murdered thousands of Jews

Massacre of Jewish, "poisoners of wells."

The church promoted the Satanization of the Jews. In this painting Satan is blindfolding a Jew so that he cannot see the truth. The truth meaning the acceptance of the true religion, Christianity.

for a crime that was never committed. In time, it became known that the water wells were not harmed by anyone. You might think that this discovery would end the persecution of our people. It didn't. The abuse and murders continued; the excuse for them changed. A pattern of hate is very difficult to change.

Books Become the Enemy

The torment of Jews living in Europe was sometimes aimed at their love of knowledge and scholarship. Books such as the Torah and Talmud were at the foundation of Judaism. These were not only studied, but they were also treasured and protected. Remember the *genizah* from chapter one? These special storage places for books show how much the Jews valued them. No wonder some Europeans believed that eliminating Jewish books and Jewish learning might also eliminate the Jewish people. So Jewish books, particularly the Talmud, were stolen from synagogues and homes. They were collected in large piles and set on fire. Sometimes there were so many books that the fire would burn for more than a day. It happened in France, Italy, and Germany as well as throughout Eastern Europe.

A Case Study

To understand more clearly what life was like for the Jews, let's look at the city of Krakow, Poland. We know that Jews settled there in the 1200s. That's 800 years ago! We also know that Jews lived there off and on for 200 years before that. Most came from Germany, or the city of Prague (now in the Czech Republic). In the beginning, life was good for the Jews. They were especially happy when King Casimir was ruler. He even issued a royal charter granting Jews the legal right to stay in Krakow. They lived on "Jewish Street," where there were many synagogues. They became merchants, traders, moneylenders, and some were even invited to be part of the

Gate of the Jewish ghetto in Vienna.

royal court. Of course, all of this only made the townspeople jealous. Trouble was on the way.

As time went on, the Jews of Krakow had to weather the Black Death and Blood Libel accusations. Each was a good excuse to riot and murder some innocent Jews. Such massacres, usually organized by the local church, were called pogroms. Gradually, the good will of the Christians in Krakow melted away. The Jews slowly lost the rights they once enjoyed. They could hold only certain jobs, and they could sell only handmade hats and collars. This must have been a difficult way to earn a living. The final blow came in 1494. The new king ruled that Jews could not stay in Krakow during the night. This meant that they could enter the city during the day, but they could no longer live there.

This decree forced the Jews of Krakow to

The medieval synagogue in Krakow. From a postcard of the mid-1930s.

move to another town, Kazimierz, which was just on the other side of the river bordering Krakow. There they settled in a small district of their own. Their population kept growing. Soon there wasn't enough space in their neighborhood to hold everyone, but the city officials wouldn't let them live anywhere else. In desperation, the leaders of the Jewish community pleaded for more land. Finally, the Jews were allowed additional space. But there was a catch. They had to buy the land at a high price and pay a yearly tax for permission to live there. Life in Europe was never easy for the Jews.

At first, walls were built around the Jewish section of the city for protection. Later, these walls were used to keep the Jews inside except for certain hours of the day. Despite these difficulties, the Jews of Kazimierz prospered. Most continued to work in Krakow. Many Jewish doctors served the king, and eventually Jewish merchants were given more rights. Although they couldn't live in Krakow, living nearby wasn't so bad. They knew that Jews in other cities had it much worse.

Krakow is just one example of how Jews lived in Europe. Each city had its own concerns. In the next section, you will learn what it was like for Jews who lived in the cities of Spain. The Spanish Jews had an unusual story. Their lives reached amazing "highs" which later dropped to terrible "lows." You won't want to miss their adventure.

YOUR JEWISH WORLD

Summarizing

During the Crusades, the Europeans became intolerant of non-Christians. They began to blame Jews for all their hardships. This intolerance resulted in Blood Libels, false accusations that Jews killed Christian children and used their blood in the making of matzah. As a result of such distrust, Jews were ordered to leave their cities or countries. Jews who did live among the Europeans were often required to wear special hats or badges. As if this were not bad enough, the Jews were also blamed for causing the horrible Black Death that spread throughout Europe during the 1300s. Pogroms—riots and massacres—were a common occurrence. Even Jewish books were burned. The lives of the Jews living in and near the city of Krakow, Poland, were typical of Jewish life in many other cities in Europe.

Understanding

Did you know that the foundation of freedom and liberty is the Magna Carta, written in England in 1215? The same ideas were used by America's founding leaders. However, did you know that these concepts were borrowed from Torah and Talmud, and were introduced to their government by English Jews?

Thinking

Think about a false rumor that hurt you or hurt someone you know. How did it make you feel? Imagine what it must have been like to be accused of the Blood Libel.

Investigating

Let's do something. Find an interesting fact on the Black Death that you can share with your class or your family.

Web Resource

Go to www.ktav.com and see the
FROM UR TO ETERNITY section

UNIT VII: Spain and the Jews

Chapter 22: The Golden Age of Spain (c. 700–1200 C.E.)

The same old story continued: Jews were trying to find countries in which they would be secure and where they could earn a living. The problem was that they could never really be sure where they would be safe since conditions were always changing. A country could be safe for a while, and then a new ruler would come along and it would be unsafe again. That is why Jews have had to move so often. There was one country, though, where Jews thrived for a long time. This country was Spain. The Jews who lived there were called Sephardim. Read on to learn about this "Golden Age" for our people.

A Surprising Friendship

In the beginning, things weren't so golden for the Jews in Spain. First, they had to deal with the Romans who were the masters there, too. You already know how unfriendly they were. When the Romans became Christians in about 300 C.E., they hated the stubborn Jews who refused to convert. Later, Spain was invaded by barbarian tribes called Visigoths. These people weren't called barbarians for nothing. Most of their kings were cruel, regularly persecuting the Jews. Things in Spain were very bad until relief came from a surprising place—the Muslims. You were already introduced to the Muslims, the followers of Muhammad, who conquered lands surrounding the Mediterranean Sea. In the year 711 C.E., the Muslims conquered most of Spain, and life for the Jews there took a turn for the better.

Conditions improved right away. At first, the Muslims in Spain, known as the Moors, were very disagreeable. Before long, though, they changed their attitude and decided to adopt a "live and let live" policy. Besides, they really needed Jewish help to fight the Christians who still controlled a small portion of land in northern Spain. These Christians were determined to

A Spanish synagogue Illuminated manuscript c. 1350.

take over the entire country. By this time, Spain was a melting pot of different peoples and cultures, and the result was a country with very creative thinking.

Variety Is the Spice of Life

Jews have always been good at learning from other cultures while maintaining their own religious identity. In Spain, they didn't isolate themselves, but instead made friends with people who had different beliefs. Because the Moors were tolerant of the Jewish religion, our people could pursue any profession they wanted. Actually, it was in the Moors' own best interest to welcome the Jews, who were the true intellectuals of the day.

It wasn't just the Muslims who encouraged the Jews to settle in their lands. Many European countries opened their doors at this time to the Jews and said "Come in." It made good sense to welcome people who were smart, motivated, and able to improve the economy. It was a great arrangement for everyone. In Spain, it marked the beginning of a glorious new age.

The Good Life

While Jews prospered in Spain for almost 500 years, the real "Golden Age" was from 900–1150 C.E. During this time, Spain became a wealthy country, both culturally and economically. The Jews were real participants in all this greatness. In those years, Jews and Muslims lived together as friends. Spain was thriving, and the Sephardic Jews were among the best and brightest of the age.

Imagine! Our people were doctors, lawyers, mathematicians, engineers, scientists, merchants, astronomers, translators, and mapmakers. They were politicians, diplomats, philosophers, poets, Rabbis, and scholars. They were so well respected that they even held high court positions in the Spanish government. The Jews were insiders, and this gave them power and prestige. As accepted members of Spanish society, they enjoyed the freedom to worship God in their own way. Their Jewish identity remained strong.

What could be better? This was truly a Golden Age. Soon, Spain would replace Babylonia as the greatest center for Jewish learning. Our people were continuing to adapt. We were passing the survival test with flying colors. With Torah, synagogues, and prayer, we could be Jewish anywhere. Spain was a beacon of Jewish culture.

With a Golden Age came "golden" people. These were men and women who made

Latin edition of the works of Isaac ben Solomon Israel, famous Jewish Tunisian physician in the 10th century. Lyons, 1515.

Abraham Zacuto (1450-1515), famous Jewish astronomer and historian, who fled Portugal to escape the Inquisition and settled in Amsterdam, Holland.

amazing contributions to society and are still remembered today. You are about to meet two of these Sephardic Jews who made a difference.

Dr. Luis Marcado, Jewish physician to the Spanish King Philip ll.

Portrait of Maimonides

An Illustration from the Mishneh Torah. The Mishneh Torah, also known as the Yad Ha-Hazakah, "Strong Hand," was the most important rabbinic work of Moses Maimonides. It consists of 14 volumes, and catalogues the subjects of all religious and legal regulations in talmudic literature.

Maimonides: A Man for All Seasons (1135–1204)

Does the name Maimonides ring a bell? Perhaps he's familiar to you because he was one of the most outstanding Jewish scholars who ever lived. It is very possible that you have one of his books on a shelf at home. His actual name was Rabbi Moshe ben Maimon. Lots of people have nicknames, but he had two of them. Rabbi Moshe ben Maimon was known as Maimonides and as Rambam. The name Rambam is the abbreviation of his Hebrew name.

Rambam was born in Cordoba, Spain in 1135. Just his luck, this was the time when conditions in Spain were becoming difficult. That's because the Moorish Empire was dying and some fanatical Muslims attacked Spain. To escape trouble, he and his family moved to Egypt. The move proved to be a good decision. In Egypt he became a brilliant physician. Soon Maimonides caught the eye of the ruler of Egypt, who made him his own personal doctor. Having such a famous patient helped Maimonides launch his career.

Practicing medicine was just one of Rambam's many professions. He was also a great philosopher and scholar. His two most popular books are still read today. One of these is called the *Mishneh Torah*. This book was a simplified version of the Talmud. Rambam knew that the average person didn't have time to read through the more than 2.5 million words that the Talmud contains. So, he highlighted all the important points in the Talmud and organized them to make the laws understandable to everyone. Can you see why such a book would be so useful?

The other famous book written by Maimonides is called Guide of the Perplexed. Perplexed means confused, so this was a book that cleared up deep questions that people had about Judaism and philosophy. This was a difficult task since religion deals with faith and philosophy deals with reason. Perhaps you, too, are a little perplexed. Maimonides discussed some difficult concepts. He was a man of many talents and is remembered as one of the greatest scholars of all times.

Judah Halevi (1075–1141)

Throughout the centuries, our people have always dreamed of returning to the Promised Land, Israel. It was especially comforting to Diaspora Jews to think about our homeland. Remembering the Covenant with God reminded Jews everywhere of their common goal. They were living in strange lands, but they believed this was temporary. Someday there would be a great homecoming. Judah Halevi was a man who dreamed such dreams. He wasn't just a dreamer, however. He expressed his feelings by writing beautiful poetry.

Title page of the Kuzari a book written by Judah Halevi, 12th-century Hebrew poet and religious philosopher.

Judah Halevi wrote over 800 poems in his lifetime, and many of them were about his one true love. Read this poem and see whether you can figure out the object of his affection:

Beautiful land
Delight of the world,
City of Kings,
My heart longs for you,
From the far-off West.
I am very sad,
When I remember how you were.
Now your glory is gone,
Your homes destroyed.
If I could fly to you
On the wings of eagles,
I would soak your soil,
With my tears.

You guessed it! It was the land of Israel. About 700 years later, the world had a name for people like Judah Halevi who loved Israel and wanted to return. They were called Zionists. The name refers to a mountain known as Zion in the heart of Jerusalem. It could be said that this famous poet was an early Zionist.

Toward the end of his life, Judah Halevi decided to make his dream of returning to Israel a reality. His timing, though, was very poor. Israel was a war-torn country. It was the time of the Crusades. Christians and Muslims were both fighting for the land, and it would be a very dangerous journey for him. He knew it would be hard crossing the rough seas and the barren desert, but he had to try. We know he got as far as Alexandria, Egypt, but he just disappeared after that. Perhaps he died at sea. One sad legend relates that he finally did reach the gates of Jerusalem. As he leaned down to kiss the holy ground of his beloved country, he was trampled to death by a horse. Whatever happened to him, we know that his poetry will live on. It even appears in our modern prayer books.

Judah Halevi and Maimonides were just two of the many brilliant Sephardic Jews who lived during this time. The Golden Age of Spain was a great period in our history. Unfortunately, it came to a bitter end. The Jews in Spain had been happy there for hundreds of years, but they were about to experience great despair. Just like the Ashkenazim, the Sephardim would also face many hardships. Soon, you will learn of the terrible persecutions they had to endure. Who would be the next tormentors? How would our people survive?

YOUR JEWISH WORLD

Summarizing

The Jews went from place to place to find a safe haven. One country, Spain, welcomed them. The Sephardic Jews who lived in Spain from 900–1150 experienced a Golden Age. For a long time under Muslim rule, they were permitted to live their lives in peace and to enjoy all professions of their choice. They became doctors, lawyers, scientists, and more. It was a time of great scholarship and prosperity. Two important individuals who made significant contributions were Maimonides and Judah Halevi.

Understanding

Did you know that seagoing men from every country used maps made by Jews? Abraham Cresques and his son Judah made the Catalan Atlas. This important atlas once belonged to the king of France and is now in the National Library in Paris. Cresques was known as Master of Maps and Compasses.

Thinking

Think about Jewish life in your country today. Could you call it a Golden Age? Why or why not?

Investigating

Let's do something. Look for books written by Maimonides in the library at your synagogue or school. You may even have some of his books on a shelf in your home.

Web Resource

Go to www.ktav.com and see the FROM UR TO ETERNITY section

Chapter 23: The Golden Age Is Over: The Persecutions Begin (c. 1200–1480 C.E.)

As you learned in Chapter 22, things were going well for the Sephardic Jews in Spain. Occasionally, however, there were riots during which religious fanatics targeted Jews. But the Jews were not worried. They ignored the many warning signs. By now you know that when a tolerant ruler was in power, life was fine, but when the ruling power changed, there could be serious problems. Well, the power in Spain changed, and the problems began.

In the last chapter you were given a clue as to the identity of the next persecutors. Do you remember reading that the Christians still controlled a small portion of land in the north of Spain while the Muslims controlled most of the country? Don't think that these Christians ever gave up the idea of making Spain their own. As a matter of fact, they were waging war all along and winning many battles against the Muslims. The Christians conquered back their land until they ruled most of Spain again. The Muslim Empire was rapidly declining. So what did this mean for the Jews?

It Was a Very Bad Year

At first, nothing really changed. The Christians encouraged the Jews to settle all over Spain. They knew that Jews were usually well educated, good businesspersons, and assets to the economy. Eventually, though, the Christians' real agenda became clear. They thought that it was their duty to make the entire world Christian. They genuinely believed that simply by accepting Jesus, a person's soul would be saved. In the beginning they asked nicely, hoping that Jews and others would see the light and embrace Christianity with open arms. But when politeness didn't work, they resorted to force. They began offering

The Muslim invaders were spurred into battle by the belief that heavenly angels protected them. The Christians adopted St. James, the Moor Killer, as their protector. He was believed to ride on a great white horse and wield a deadly sword. This Spanish painting pictures St. James in battle with the Moors.

the Jews the choice of becoming Christians or facing death. What a terrible choice to have to make! Many people converted. They were called New Christians or Conversos. Remember the word "Converso." You will see it again.

Unfortunately, 1391 was a very bad year. Riots broke out all over Spain and it was open season for killing Jews. The Jewish communities of Toledo, Seville, and Cordoba were especially hit hard. During this time, thousands of our

The city of Granada in Southern Spain was the last outpost of Moorish control. It was captured by the Christians in 1492. This painting shows Ferdinand and Isabella triumphantly entering the city.

No Arguing with the Church

There were rumblings of trouble with the Church in Spain for a long time. In its effort to show its superiority, the Church frequently held debates to prove which was the true religion—Judaism or Christianity. These debates were known as Disputations. The most famous one occurred in 1263 in Barcelona. A great Sephardic Jewish scholar named Nachmanides was forced to debate against the claim that Jesus was the Messiah. Nachmanides reminded the Christians that the Messiah was to come only when there was peace on earth. Clearly, they all had to admit that there was no peace. Still, the Church was powerful and had final authority. Nachmanides was banished from Spain as punishment for such a wise debate.

people were murdered or forcibly converted to Christianity.

Before going any farther, something needs to be very clear. The Christians we are discussing lived hundreds of years ago during the Middle Ages. We are not talking about your Christian friends and neighbors today. Times were very different then, and you are learning about the past.

Seal of Nachmanides found near the city of Acre.

A medieval artist's idea of a discussion between Christians and Jews.

Another favorite pastime of the Church involved placing the Talmud on trial. Can you imagine anything more ridiculous than putting a book on trial? If the Jews defended the Talmud too well, they could be killed. If they didn't defend it well enough, they were disloyal to their beliefs. What a predicament. Sadly, these kinds of trials happened in Spain and then all over Europe.

It was a horrible time in our history. We had survived so much adversity for so many years. Our belief in the Covenant with God remained strong. But there were forces working to destroy us that were beyond our control. We were few in number; the Christians were many. They were strong and powerful. And they were in charge.

This altar relief shows the forced conversion of Jewish women. The women were forced to choose between conversion and exile.

Isabella and Ferdinand witness the conversion of a Jew. Note that the kneeling Jew has crossed his arms into the shape of a cross.

Hard Choices

For many Jews in Spain, it was a time of decision. What would they do? One choice was to remain Jewish and to take their chances. Many of our people did just that. They tried to go about their lives and be inconspicuous, hoping not to be noticed. It was a dangerous way to live. Others tried to find countries where Jews were accepted. This was getting more difficult, however, as the influence of the Church grew in Europe. In addition, it wasn't easy to pack up and leave a country where your family had been living for hundreds of years. Unfortunately, many thousands of our people made another choice. They actually converted to Christianity and were lost to Judaism forever.

The "Secret Jews"

There was one other option. Many of the Jews in Spain decided to be practical. They were committed to their religion, but they didn't want to die. So, they pretended to become "New Christians." They went through conversion and, in public, acted as if they were Christians. In their hearts and homes, however, they were still practicing Jews. The Christians called these secret Jews "Marranos." In Spanish, this is an insult, since the word means "pig." These secret Jews observed Shabbat and the holidays, and continued to have Jewish weddings and circumcisions in secret. Of course, they lived in fear of discovery, and had to be careful to hide these activities from their neighbors. Many of them had escape plans. It was not uncommon to have secret passageways that led from a house or synagogue to the street in case a quick getaway was necessary.

Thousands of Sephardic Jews became New Christians. It appeared that the "forced conversion program" was working well. The Church was happy that a lot of souls were being "saved." Difficulties arose when the New Christians began competing with the Old Christians for important positions in the Church. Since the Church had to recognize these Conversos with no strings attached, it caused a lot of jealousy and hard feelings.

To add to this frustration, rumors were flying that many of these Conversos were hiding their Judaism. It was discovered that some of these secret Jews were even holding high positions in the Spanish government. This was completely unacceptable. The Church had to solve this problem, but didn't know how to find all these false Christians. The church had created its own nightmare. A foolproof system for hunting down the offenders had to be devised. Ironically, instead of going after Jews who refused to convert, all the attention was focused on the secret Jews, whom they called heretics, or unfaithful Christians.

The Inquisition

The Church went after the secret Jews with great passion. It hunted them down like animals. It became a mission to find these insincere

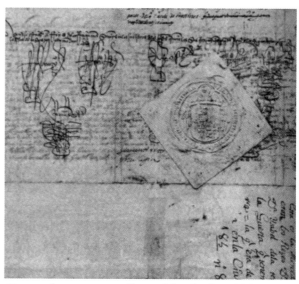

Grant of property, confiscated by the Inquisition, to a Christian monastery, by Ferdinand and Isabella (autographed).

Christians, force them to confess their devotion to Judaism, and punish them. Thus began one of the darkest times in the history of the Jews. It was called the Inquisition. Its purpose was to find and punish those Conversos who were practicing Judaism in secret. The Inquisition was not new to Europe, but in about 1480, it became new to Spain. This country used it in a unique and treacherous way.

A No-Win Situation

Here's how the Inquisition worked. Committees of churchmen were given the task of flushing out heretics and "bringing them to justice." The so-called heretics were put on trial, but they were never given the opportunity to defend themselves. Picture this. If you were suspected of being a heretic, or unfaithful Christian, someone might come for you in the middle of the night. You would be carried off from your home and thrown into prison. You might never see your family again. Most of the time, you didn't even know your accusers. If you survived the diseases, malnutrition, and miserable conditions of the prison, you would be brought to trial. You would be ordered to confess your true beliefs. If you claimed your innocence, you would be tortured until you did confess. People were so frightened of the authorities that they would occasionally betray their own family members to escape torture.

In fear of such punishment, many secret Jews didn't even tell their own children that they were Jewish. If a small child revealed this information to friends, the whole family would be in danger. Perhaps the child's Jewish identity would be disclosed for the first time when he or she became a teenager.

Guilty, but Never Proven Innocent

What was the punishment for being a heretic? It wasn't always the same for everyone. If a person confessed to this "crime," sometimes he or she was given another chance to be a "real" Christian. Such returning Conversos were always under careful watch. No one really trusted them. Frequently, though, the heretics would be severely punished for their sins even if they confessed. Some were forced to work on ships. Others were thrown into dungeons for years. Their property would be taken, and their children would be tormented.

Confessions were not always easy to get. The Covenant with God still lived in the people's hearts. Their faith made them strong even in the face of torture. In the next chapter you will meet one of the most evil villains in history and discover what he did to earn this terrible reputation.

YOUR JEWISH WORLD

Summarizing

The Golden Age of Spain drew to a close as the Christians began to conquer back the land. These Christians tried to convert people of other religions, and especially targeted the Jews. Jews were given the choice of fleeing Spain, conversion, or death. Riots broke out, and Jewish communities lived in fear. At this time, some Jews did convert, but many pretended to become Christians while remaining Jewish in secret. Many of these secret Jews rose to high government and Church positions. The Church attempted to find these heretics and punish them. That is why the Inquisition started in Spain. A time of great persecution was about to begin.

Understanding

Did you know that Marco Polo wasn't the only great world traveler? One hundred years before Marco Polo, a Jew named Benjamin of Tudela visited over 300 places in France, Italy, Greece, Palestine, Iraq, the Persian Gulf, Egypt, and Sicily. He wrote about his travels in a book published in 1543.

Thinking

Think about how you would have handled the difficult times in Spain. Would you have practiced Judaism openly, become a secret Jew, left for another place to live, or converted to Christianity? Explain the reasons for your choice.

Investigating

Let's do something. Write a story about a boy or girl who lived as a secret Jew in Spain during the Spanish Inquisition.

Web Resource

Go to www.ktav.com and see the **FROM UR TO ETERNITY** section

Chapter 24: Forced Out of Spain: New Challenges (c. 1480–1550 C.E.)

The Inquisition was feared by every Jew. The Church had a special treatment for the Jews who proclaimed their innocence to the end. Church officials wanted to make examples out of those who refused to cooperate. With this in mind, they introduced the ultimate punishment, the auto-da-fé. The actual meaning of this term is "act of faith."

During special Christian holidays, the main square of a city was prepared for the auto-da-fé. Thousands were invited to attend. The excitement was felt by everyone, as they awaited a great spectacle like a sporting event. However, it was not to be a football match or a baseball game. Instead, they would see the actual punishment of secret Jews who were "convicted" of being heretics. They would watch these people being burned alive at the stake. Isn't it ironic that killing someone cruelly and unjustly could be called an "act of faith?"

Trial by Fire

Picture a gigantic stadium filled with people. The royalty and nobility sat in a special section so they would have the best view. Church leaders marched in first as if in a parade. After them came those who were condemned to die. The convicted people wore yellow tunics with different pictures and symbols revealing their "crime." Each carried a candle. A priest delivered a sermon that warned about the evils of being a heretic, an unfaithful Christian. Then the punishments were announced. The crowd cheered. Those whose punishment was death by fire were led to the scaffold. Then the king, or another important individual, lit the fire. It was considered an honor to carry out this task.

Two Jews await their fate at the auto-da-fé. Note the holiday atmosphere and notables in the viewing stands. In the foreground are two costumed Sanbenitos, victims of the Inquisition who are shown being converted by a priest holding a cross.

The auto-da-fé was often saved for special celebrations such as births, weddings, or Christian holidays. Believe it or not, a king of Spain, Charles II, even presented his wife Marie Louise with a wedding gift—prime seats at an auto-da-fé at the grand plaza of Madrid. On that occasion, 51 people were burned at the stake. We know that many thousands of Jews were murdered this way during the Inquisition. It is hard to imagine how this horrible spectacle could have been enjoyed by the onlookers.

A King and Queen Wearing Several Hats

Let's talk about those who were in charge of such atrocities. Who was responsible for bringing the Inquisition and the auto-da-fé to Spain? Two important individuals in this scheme were King Ferdinand and Queen Isabella. These names probably sound familiar to you, because they were the rulers of Spain who sent Christopher Columbus to look for a trade route to India. They are the very same king and queen who welcomed the Inquisition into their country. Here's what happened.

In the year 1474, Ferdinand and Isabella became king and queen of Spain. Because Isabella was such a devout Christian, she wanted the whole country to believe as she did. At that time, there were still many Jews and Muslims in Spain. She was especially frustrated with the secret Jews she believed were ruining the purity of the Church. It was her idea to bring the Inquisition to Spain. She was hoping to rid the country of all "unwanted" people.

Cruel acts require cruel people to carry them out. Because Ferdinand and Isabella were busy with their royal duties, they appointed Tomás de Torquemada to be the Grand Inquisitor. Torquemada was a Christian monk. He was a cruel, evil, and fanatical man. He taught his people how to trap and torture heretics. For example, a Converso who refused to eat pork was immediately arrested. Often surprise visits would be made during Shabbat or Jewish holidays to catch people in the "act of being Jewish."

A Stern Decree

While the Inquisition was a very effective tool for hunting down and punishing heretics, the truth was that it was getting harder to manage. Such an operation required a lot of labor and paperwork. It was taking too much time away from Church duties. Because Torquemada was a practical tyrant, he had to come up with a better

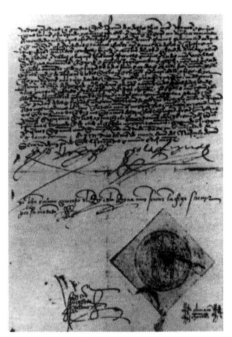

Edict of Expulsion, bearing seal and signature of the Catholic kings, Granada, March 31, 1492.

idea. He decided that the only way to rid Spain of the problem was to rid Spain of the Jews. Suddenly, the solution seemed simple. Torquemada approached the king and queen with his plan. He argued that the New Christians were constantly being influenced by their Jewish friends and neighbors. If all the Jews were to leave the country, it would be so much easier to keep an eye on the New Christians. Temptation would be removed.

At first, Ferdinand and Isabella didn't approve the plan. They felt that the Jews were too important to the economy. Money was needed to conquer Granada, the last holdout of the Muslims. Then, in 1492, the Muslims surrendered at Granada. The entire country was now Christian. Torquemada's timing was excellent. He eagerly approached the king and queen again with his solution. Now, his proposition interested them. The Jews were given a choice. Either they converted to Christianity, or they had to leave Spain forever. Isaac Abrabanel, a Jew and chief finance minister to Ferdinand and Isabella, tried unsuccessfully to change their minds. Torquemada's influence on them was too strong. On March 31, 1492, the king and queen signed the Edict of Expulsion. All Jews were to leave Spain by August 1 of that year. They had just four months to gather all their belongings and make their arrangements.

Homeless Again

In Chapter 15, you learned that the First and Second Temples were destroyed on the same day of the year, and that Jews observe that day as Tishah B'Av. In Spain, about 1400 years after the Second Temple fell, that date became unlucky again. August 1, 1492 happened to be Tishah B'Av. Could Ferdinand and Isabella have known this was a time of mourning for our people? Did they plan it that way? Who knows? Meanwhile, the Jewish people were heartsick. They had always considered themselves good Spanish citizens. Suddenly, they were no longer welcome there. They were being thrown out of their own country!

After living in Spain for over a thousand years, the Jews prepared to leave. They weren't permitted to take gold or silver. Their property was sold for practically nothing. Perhaps they received a mule in exchange for their house, or a piece of cloth for their vineyard. Most had to travel by donkey or on foot. Jews who could afford passage on a ship risked being thrown overboard by greedy sea captains who stole their possessions. Those who were ill or too weak for travel died on route to their destination.

On the Run

In the end, over 200,000 Jews left Spain. The most obvious destination was Portugal. If you look on a map, you will see how close Portugal is to Spain. Portugal provided only a temporary solution, though, because five years later the Jews were forced to leave there as well. The Sephardic

Isaac Abrabanel

Jews found new homes wherever they could. Mostly, they stayed in areas around the Mediterranean Sea. They went to such places we now call North Africa, Syria, Egypt, Turkey, France, Italy, Holland, and, of course, Israel.

Jews also made their way to the New World. You are familiar with Christopher Columbus's famous voyage. Did you also know that there may have been secret Jews sailing on his ship? There is even a rumor that Christopher Columbus himself was a Converso. This hasn't been proven, but there is some pretty convincing evidence that at least one of his ancestors was Jewish. The Jews were expelled on Tishah B'Av. Columbus set sail the next day. Could he have delayed his departure because he was observing the Jewish day of mourning? Was this just a coincidence? (Surely you know how important the year 1492 is for Americans. Now you know how important it was for the Jews of Spain.)

Try to imagine what it was like for the Sephardic Jews. Spain had the largest Jewish population in Europe at the time, and now they were forced to scatter. They had to make a new home in strange lands. Once again, they would have to

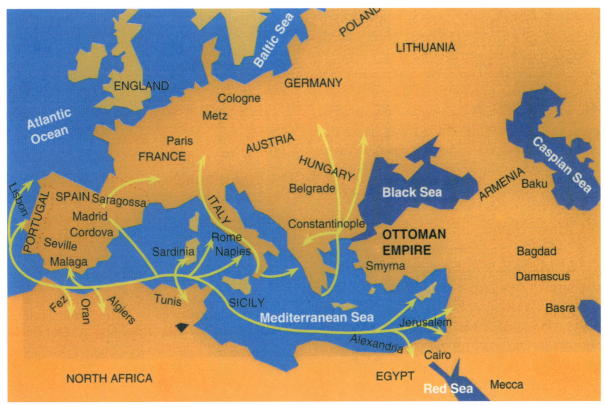

The expulsion from Spain in 1492. The map shows how the first exiles went to Portugal and Southern Italy; persecution followed and many fled eastward to countries of the Ottoman Empire.

adapt to new languages, cultures, and neighbors. It wasn't easy.

You may be interested to know that the first Jews who settled in the United States were Sephardim. Here's what took place. Some of the Jews who left Spain fled to Recife, Brazil, in South America. As a Dutch colony, it was a safe place, where Jews were treated very well. That changed when Brazil was conquered by the Portuguese. The Jews fled to the north. Twenty-three of them landed in New Amsterdam in 1654. You know this place better by its modern name—New York!

No More Secrecy

You might be wondering what happened to all the Jews who had pretended to convert to Christianity. Theirs is an interesting story. At first, they were able to preserve many of their Jewish traditions. In secret they still observed the holidays and continued to teach their children about Judaism. But, each generation knew less than the last one. Eventually, people couldn't remember why they observed certain Jewish rituals, so many stopped doing them. The Jews had tried so hard to keep their faith, but the secrecy made it almost impossible for them to continue. Before long, many forgot that they were Jewish. Can you see how that could happen?

Even in the United States today, we have evidence of the effect of the Spanish Inquisition. We can find it in the Southwest, the area once settled by Spanish explorers. A number of people living in New Mexico, Arizona, and parts of Colorado are descendants of Conversos. They grew up as Christians, but, oddly enough, some Jewish rituals have survived in their homes for over 500 years. Some light candles on Friday evening. Some of their gravestones are marked with a Magen David (Star of David) or a menorah. Some learned of their origins from their parents or grandparents. Others continued these practices even without knowing why. As they learn more of the facts about their Jewish ancestry, many are eager to return to their Jewish roots. Thankfully, there is no reason for secrecy anymore.

A Culture Shock

The Jews weren't the only ones hurt by the Edict of Expulsion. The Spanish people were also hurt by this terrible act. Hundreds of thousands of well-educated Jews left the country, taking with them their outstanding talents and vibrant culture. Spain would never again be the thriving country it had been when the Jews were there. During the Golden Age, almost half the Jewish population in the world lived in Spain. Then, suddenly, they were gone. This loss took its toll on Spain.

It may be hard to believe, but the Edict of Expulsion was not formally revoked until 1968! Even though Jews were free to return long before that, it wasn't a friendly atmosphere for them. In 1992, the king of Spain actually apologized for his ancestors' expulsion of the Jews 500 years before.

Just as surprising, on March 15, 2000, Pope John Paul II issued an apology for sins committed by the Church against the Jews. He set up a commission to look into the actions of the Church, and for the first time allowed historians to study the records of the Inquisition. At last, the Church realized that an accurate understanding of the past is essential to leading a moral Christian life.

The End is Not Near

When Solomon's Temple was destroyed, the Jewish people found a new life in Babylonia. Because of their commitment to God, they adapted, realizing that is was possible to be Jewish away from home. When the second Temple was destroyed, they scattered, and again learned to adapt to their new situation. The Sephardic Jews of Spain faced the same difficulties of survival. As they settled in other countries, they continued to practice their Judaism. The Covenant still lived in their hearts and minds. Jewish survival skills were becoming very strong indeed.

Don't think that the story of the Spanish Jews ended with their expulsion from Spain. No. There is a whole lot more to learn about them—just as there is a whole lot more to learn about all the Jews in the Diaspora. In Part II the historical adventures of the Jews continue.

TISHA B'AV-NINTH OF AV

TRAGEDY	ENEMY	DATE	LEADER
1ST. TEMPLE	BABYLON	586 B.C.E.	NEBUCHADNEZZAR
2ND. TEMPLE	ROME	70 C.E.	TITUS
EXPULSION	SPAIN	1492	TORQUEMADA

Pope John Paul II at the Western Wall in Jerusalem begs for forgiveness for the sins committed against the Jews.

YOUR JEWISH WORLD

Summarizing

When King Ferdinand and Queen Isabella became the rulers of Spain in 1474, they brought the Inquisition to their country. They also made Tomás de Torquemada the Grand Inquisitor. This was one of the worst times in Jewish history. Secret Jews who did not confess to heresy would be burned alive at the auto-da-fé. Thousands were murdered this way. Eventually, the Jews were given a choice, either convert, or be expelled from Spain. At this time many converted to Christianity, but about 200,000 Jews departed. Some may have sailed with Christopher Columbus. The Jews who left Spain were known as Sephardim. Mostly they settled in countries along the Mediterranean Sea, but some eventually arrived in America. They developed their own culture and traditions while maintaining their Covenant with God.

Understanding

Did you know that Christopher Columbus once saved himself and his crew from trouble by predicting a solar eclipse? He used the astronomical charts prepared by the Jewish astronomer, Abraham Zacuto.

Thinking

Think about how you would feel if you were forced to leave your homeland. How would you decide where to go? What would you take with you?

Investigating

Let's do something. Do some research on Christopher Columbus. Use books, the Internet, and magazine articles. Can you find some facts that show he might have been Jewish?

Web Resource

Go to www.ktav.com and see the
FROM UR TO ETERNITY section

Chapter 25: Epilogue

Our story began about 4,000 years ago when God made a special Brit, or Covenant, with a man named Abraham. God promised to protect Abraham and his children. In return, Abraham and his children promised to believe in and obey God. This partnership has remained the foundation of Judaism.

Our relationship with God has been tested throughout many adventures. We met tough challenges, yet the partnership has never been broken. Let's review. Long ago we were slaves in Egypt. When finally free we were surrounded by enemies in the Promised Land. We built a mighty empire under our kings, Saul, David, and Solomon, only to have it conquered. The Babylonians, Persians, Greeks, and Romans ruled over us. Our Temples were destroyed. Our people were scattered to unknown lands where Christians or Muslims were in control. Our future was uncertain and the road was always bumpy. Through it all we have moved on and lived on.

Life dealt us some hard blows, but we maintained a strong Jewish spirit. Along the way many good things happened to us. Just look at how we were able to form a tight bond and become a people both with and without a homeland. Because our religion taught us right from wrong, we showed others by example how to be caring, kind, and fair. Our communities and families became strong. Our children were educated. They became outstanding scientists, doctors, inventors, writers, diplomats, and merchants. We can be proud!

We can also be proud of our ability to adapt to difficult situations. We adapted our rituals and practices so we could be Jewish anywhere. Without our beloved Temple we substituted synagogues and prayers. We wrote down our Oral Law, which became known as the Talmud. Rabbis became our teachers so that we never lost the wisdom of the Torah. We adapted as a people by gaining from each of our conquerors without losing our own identity. For example, we appreciated the great thinkers of Greece without praying to their gods. We learned from the brilliant scholars of Spain without becoming Muslims. It seems our constant hardships have made us better.

The Diaspora changed the lives of our people forever. They were forced to take different paths. Some Jews lived in the Christian-controlled countries of Europe. They were called Ashkenazim. Others lived in the Muslim-controlled areas around the Mediterranean Sea. They were called Sephardim. Both have their own stories to tell.

When we last left the Ashkenazim they were living complicated lives. Time and again they suffered the pressure of being different from their Christian neighbors. No country felt like home. Things were no better for the Sephardim. Despite their early comfort in Spain, the situation turned bad. It all ended when they were kicked out of the country that had been their home for hundreds of years.

We will pause now in our story. Many adventures will follow in Part II. Our people were headed for more surprises. Many would be forced to live in cities with walls separating them from the outside world. While they would suffer, their lives would also be filled with moments of joy. You will meet men like the Ba'al Shem Tov, who came up with a whole new way to be Jewish in troubled times. You will also meet women like Doña Gracia Mendes, a secret Jew who helped others escape the terrible Inquisition.

As the adventures continue, our people will face new challenges. We will remain strong. No matter what happens, we will never forget our everlasting connection to God.

Index

Abrabanel, Isaac, 105
Abraham, 6, 8-15, 22, 82
Absalom, 29
Adam, 6
Ahab, 37
Akiva, Rabbi, 74
Alexander the Great, 51
Ammonites, 26
Amos, 38
Antiochus, 55-56
Arameans, 28
Ark of the Covenant, 18, 32, 42
Ashkenazim, 82-83, 84-93
Assyrians, 38
Atlas (Greek god), 53

Baal the idol, 21, 37
Babylonia, 39-50, 73-75
Babylonians, 40-47
Barak, 23
Bet HaMikdash, See: Temple
Black Death, 91-92
Blood Libel, 90
Brit, See: Covenant

Caleb, 19
Canaanites, 20-23
Casimir, King of Poland, 92
Christianity, 76-77, 80-82, 84-87, 89-91, 94, 99-108
Columbus, Christopher, 2, 5, 105, 106
Conversos, See: Marranos
Covenant with God, 9-15, 17, 20-22, 38-40, 43-44, 47, 81-82, 97, 101, 103, 108
Crusades, 89, 98
Cyrus the Great, 47-48, 73

David, 26-30
Dead Sea, 67
Deborah, 23
Delilah, 23
Disputations, 100

Edomites, 26, 28
Eleazar ben Yair, 68
Elijah, 38
Esau, 13
Euphrates River, 42

Eve, 6
Exiguus, Dionysius, 5, 7
Exodus, 2, 17
Ezekiel, 43, 45-46, 48

Ezra, 49-50
Ferdinand, King of Spain, 105-106
Florus, 63

Gabriel, 78
Ge'onim, 73
Gemara, 74
genizah, 3-4, 92
Gideon, 22
Golden Calf, 18
Goliath, 27
Greeks, 51-52

Hagar, 12
Hasmoneans, 57-61
Hellenists, 53, 55, 59, 83
Herod, 62-63, 65, 67
Hillel, 72-73
Hiram, King of Tyre, 31

Inquisition, 102-106, 108
Isaac, 12-13, 15
Isabella, Queen of Spain, 105-106
Isaiah, 38-39, 43, 48
Ishmael, 12
Islam, 77-80, 81-82, 89, 94-99

Jabin, 23
Jacob, 13-15
Jason, 55
Jeremiah, 39, 43
Jericho, 20
Jeroboam, 36
Jesus, 5, 6, 76-77, 89, 100
Jezebel, 37
Jocheved, 16
Jonathan, 27
Joseph, 13, 15-16
Josephus, 68-69
Joshua, 19-20
Josiah, 40
Judah ha Nasi, 74
Judah Halevi, 97-98
Judah Maccabee, 57
Judges, 21-25

Kazimierz, Poland, 93
Kohanim, 39
Kohen Gadol, 39, 51, 55, 58
Koran, 78
Krakow, Poland, 92-93

Leah, 13, 15
Levites, 39

Maimonides, 96-98
manna, 17
Marranos, 2, 99, 101-108
Masada, 62, 67-69
Mattathias, 56-57
matzah, 17, 90
Mecca, 77-79
Medina, 78-79
Menelaus, 55
Messiah, 76-77
Michal, 27
Midianites, 22
Mishkan, 18, 32, 39
Mishnah, 74
Moabites, 26, 28
Modin, 56
Moors, 94
Moses, 2, 16-20, 22
Mount Nebo, 20
Mount Sinai, 2, 17-18
Mount Tabor, 23
Muhammad, 6
Muhammad, 77-79, 94
Muslim, See: Islam

Naboth, 37,
Nachmanides, 100
Nathan, 30
Nebuchadnezzar, 40-42, 73, 83
Nehemiah, 49-50
New Christians, See: Marranos
Nile River, 16

Oral Law, 59, 74

Paul, 77
Persians, 47-50
Pharaoh, 14-15, 16-17, 30
Pharisees, 58-59
Philistines, 23-24, 26-28, 62
plagues, 17
pogroms, 92
Pompey, 61-63
Pope John Paul II, 108-109
Prophets, 24, 37-40
Ptolemy the Second, 52
Ptolemy, 51
Rachel, 13, 15
Rahab, 20

Rambam, See: Maimonides
Rashi, 85
Rebecca, 12-13, 15
Rehoboam, 35
Romans, 61-70, 76-77

Sadducees, 58-59
Samaritans, 49
Samson, 23-24
Samuel, 24-27
Sanhedrin, 72, 88
Sarah, 9, 11-12, 15
Saul, 26-27
Seleucus, 51
Sephardim, 82-83, 94-108
Septuagint, 52
Sheba, Queen of, 31
Shoftim, See: Judges
Silva, 68
Sisera, 23
Solomon, 30-36, 41, 45
Spain, 94-109
spies, 19
Syrian Greeks, 56-57

Tabernacle, See: Mishkan
Talmud, 74, 83, 92, 97, 101
Temple,
First, 32-33, 40-42, 45, 83
Second, 47-49, 55-57, 61-66, 70
Ten Commandments, 2, 17-18
Ten Lost Tribes of Israel, 38
Tishah B'Av, 40, 66, 106
Titus, 63-65
Torquemada, Tomás de, 105-106
Tosafists, 85

Ur, 8-11, 40
Valley of Gihon, 30
Vespasian, 63, 69-70
Visigoths, 94

Western Wall, 65

Yadin, Yigael, 68
Yael the Kenite, 23
Yavneh, 70, 83
Yochanan ben Zakkai, 69-70, 83

Zadok, 30
Zealots, 63-64, 67-69
Zeus (Greek god), 56